Enhancing Learning through Formative Assessment and Feedback

Providing feedback to students is an important aspect of the teacher's role in higher education. It enables students to learn from assessment and can have a significant impact on the motivation of a learner, both intrinsic (wanting to learn) and extrinsic (needing to learn). This book suggests that the quality and timeliness of feedback are key features in the student learning process and in the teacher/student relationship.

By encouraging teachers to think about what it is they are trying to achieve in providing formative assessment and feedback, and how these provide an enhanced learning environment for students, *Enhancing Learning through Formative Assessment and Feedback* aims to improve student learning opportunities in higher education. Topics discussed include:

- principles of formative assessment and feedback
- the student learning environment
- formative assessment and feedback techniques
- making use of ICTs in formative assessment and feedback
- benefits of formative feedback for academic staff.

Enhancing Learning through Formative Assessment and Feedback applies relevant theories and principles through teaching scenarios and case studies to create a pragmatic framework and set of tools that will allow teachers to engage with students through formative activities. It will appeal to new and experienced teachers in higher and further education, as well as professional developers.

Alastair Irons is Associate Dean in the School of Computing, Engineering and Information Sciences at Northumbria University.

Key Guides for Effective Teaching in Higher Education Series
Edited by Kate Exley

This indispensable series is aimed at new lecturers, post-graduate students who have teaching time, Graduate Teaching Assistants, part-time tutors and demonstrators, as well as experienced teaching staff who may feel it's time to review their skills in teaching and learning.

Titles in this series will provide the teacher in higher education with practical, realistic guidance on the various different aspects of their teaching role, which is underpinned not only by current research in the field, but also by the extensive experience of individual authors, and with a keen eye kept on the limitations and opportunities therein. By bridging a gap between academic theory and practice, all titles will provide generic guidance on teaching, learning and assessment issues, which is then brought to life through the use of short illustrative examples drawn from a range of disciplines. All titles in the series will:

- represent up-to-date thinking and incorporate the use of computing and information technology (C&IT) where appropriate
- consider methods and approaches for teaching and learning when there is an increasing diversity in learning and a growth in student numbers
- encourage reflexive practice and self-evaluation, and a means of developing the skills of teaching, learning and assessment
- provide links and references to other work on the topic and research evidence where appropriate.

Titles in the series will prove invaluable whether they are used for self-study or as part of a formal induction programme on teaching in higher education (HE), and will also be of relevance to teaching staff working in further education (FE) settings.

Other titles in this series:

Assessing Skills and Practice
  – Sally Brown and Ruth Pickford
Assessing Students' Written Work: Marking Essays and Reports
  – Catherine Haines
Designing Learning: From Module Outline to Effective Teaching
  – Chris Butcher, Clara Davies and Melissa Highton
Developing Your Teaching: Ideas, Insight and Action
  – Peter Kahn and Lorraine Walsh
Giving a Lecture: From Presenting to Teaching
  – Kate Exley and Reg Dennick
Small Group Teaching
  – Kate Exley and Reg Dennick
Using C&IT to Support Teaching
  – Paul Chin

Enhancing Learning through Formative Assessment and Feedback

Alastair Irons

Routledge
Taylor & Francis Group

LONDON AND NEW YORK

First published 2008
by Routledge
2 Park Square, Milton Park, Abingdon, Oxon OX14 4RN

Simultaneously published in the USA and Canada
by Routledge
711 Third Avenue, New York, NY 10017

Routledge is an imprint of the Taylor & Francis Group, an informa business

Typeset in Perpetua by
Florence Production Ltd, Stoodleigh, Devon

British Library Cataloguing in Publication Data
A catalogue record for this book is available from the British Library

Library of Congress Cataloging in Publication Data
Irons, Alastair, 1962–
    Enhancing learning through formative assessment/Alastair Irons.
        p. cm. – (Key guides for effective teaching in higher
        education series)
        Includes bibliographical references and index.
    1. Educational tests and measurements.   2. Feedback
(Psychology)   3. Education, Higher.   I. Title.
LB3051.I76 2007
371.27′1–dc22   2007013941

ISBN13: 978–0–415–39780–3 (hbk)
ISBN13: 978–0–415–39781–0 (pbk)
ISBN13: 978–0–203–93433–3 (ebk)

To my darling
son, Sam

Contents

List of illustrations   viii
Series preface   ix
Acknowledgements   xii
List of abbreviations   xiii

Introduction   1

1   Principles of formative assessment and formative feedback   6

2   Student learning environment   31

3   Using formative assessment and formative feedback in
    learning and teaching   52

4   Formative assessment and feedback techniques   70

5   Making use of ICTs in formative assessment and formative
    feedback   87

6   Benefits of formative feedback for academic staff   98

7   Case studies   108

8   Summary and recommendations   135

References   140
Index   151

Illustrations

FIGURES

7.1	Effectiveness of initiative: student outcome	114
7.2	PASS attendance	117
7.3	A typical KELPIE screen	120
7.4	Marking categories template	123
7.5	The examination board Collection procedure	130

TABLES

7.1	Effectiveness of initiative: student attrition rates	112
7.2	Effectiveness of initiative: student recruitment	116
7.3	Marking categories	121

Series preface

This series of books grew out of discussions with new lecturers and part-time teachers in universities and colleges who were keen to develop their teaching skills. However, experienced colleagues may also enjoy and find merit in the books, particularly the discussions about current issues that are impacting on teaching and learning in further education (FE) and higher education (HE), e.g. Widening Participation, disability legislation and the integration of computing and information technology (C&IT) in teaching.

New lecturers are now likely to be required by their institutions to take part in teaching development programmes. This frequently involves attending workshops, investigating teaching through mini-projects and reflecting on their practice. Many teaching programmes ask participants to develop their own teaching portfolios and to provide evidence of their developing skills and understanding. Scholarship of teaching is usually an important aspect of the teaching portfolio. New teachers can be asked to consider their own approach to teaching in relation to the wider literature, research findings and theory of teaching and learning. However, when people are beginning their teaching careers a much more pressing need may be to design and deliver an effective teaching session for tomorrow. Hence the intention of this series is to provide a complementary mix of very practical teaching tips and guidance together with a strong basis and clear rationale for their use.

In many institutions the numbers of part-time and occasional teachers actually outnumber the full-time staff. Yet the provision of formal training and development for part-time teachers is more sporadic and variable across the sector. As a result, this diverse group of educators can feel isolated and left out of the updating and support offered to their full-time counterparts. Never have there been so many part-time teachers involved in the design and delivery of courses, the support and guidance of students and the monitoring and assessment of learning. The group includes the thousands of post-graduate students who work as lab-demonstrators, problem class tutors, project supervisors and class teachers. The group includes clinicians, lawyers and professionals who contribute their specialist knowledge and skills to enrich the learning experience for many vocational and professional course students. The group also includes the many hourly paid and jobbing tutors who have helped full-time staff cope with the expansion and diversification of HE and FE.

Universities sometimes struggle to know how many part-time staff they employ to teach and, as a group, occasional teachers are notoriously difficult to systematically contact through university and college communication systems. Part-time and occasional teachers often have other roles and responsibilities and teaching is a small but important part of what they do each day. Many part-time tutors would not expect to undertake the full range of teaching activities of full-time staff but may well do lots of tutoring or lots of class teaching but never lecture, or supervise (or vice versa). So the series provides short practical books focusing very squarely on different teaching roles and activities. The first four books published are:

- *Assessing Students' Written Work: Marking Essays and Reports*
- *Giving a Lecture: From Presenting to Teaching*
- *Small Group Teaching*
- *Using C&IT to Support Teaching*

The books are all very practical with detailed discussion of teaching techniques and methods but they are based upon educational theory and research findings. Articles are referenced, further readings and related web sites are given and workers in the field are quoted and acknowledged. To this end Dr George Brown has been commissioned to produce an associated web-based guide on Student Learning which can be freely accessed by readers to accompany the books and provide a substantial foundation for the teaching and assessment practices discussed and recommended for the texts.

There is much enthusiasm and support here too for the excellent work currently being carried out by the Higher Education Academy subject centres within discipline groupings (indeed, individual subject centres are suggested as sources of further information throughout these volumes). The need to provide part-time tutors with realistic connections with their own disciplines is keenly felt by all the authors in the series and 'how it might work in your department' examples are given at the end of many of the activity-based chapters. However, there is no doubt some merit in sharing teaching developments across the boundaries of disciplines, culture and country as many of the problems in the tertiary education sector are themselves widely shared.

UNDERLYING THEMES

The use of computing and information technology to enrich student learning and to help manage the workload of teachers is a recurring theme in the series. I acknowledge that not all teachers may yet have access to state-of-the-art teaching resources and facilities. However, the use of Virtual Learning Environments (VLEs), e-learning provision and audio-visual presentation media is now widespread in universities.

The books also acknowledge and try to help new teachers respond to the growing and changing nature of the student population. Students with non-traditional backgrounds, international students, students who have disabilities or special needs are encouraged through the government's Widening Participation agenda to take part in further and higher education. The books seek to advise teachers on current legislative requirements and offer guidance on recommended good practice on teaching diverse groups of students.

These were our goals and I and my co-authors sincerely hope these volumes prove to be a helpful resource for colleagues, both new and experienced, in higher education.

Acknowledgements

I would like to thank all my colleagues and friends who gave so freely of their time and advice and were happy to share experiences of formative assessment and formative feedback. Particular thanks are due to those colleagues who very kindly prepared case studies – which are included in Chapter 7. Thanks to all the students who have directly and indirectly contributed to this book through their comments, experiences and participation in formative activities.

Thanks also to colleagues at Northumbria University, especially those in the School of Computing, Engineering and Information Sciences, the Assessment Enhancement Group and my fellow Associate Deans for Learning and Teaching all of whom have provided encouragement, advice and support. Thanks to Kate Exley as editor of this series whose encouragement, advice and support have been invaluable. And an extra special thanks to my two boys – for it is the feedback dialogue that we engage in that is the most enjoyable, satisfying and rewarding.

Abbreviations

AfL	Assessment for Learning
C&IT	computing and information technology
CBA	computer based assessment
CETL	Centre for Excellence in Teaching and Learning
CTI	Computers in Teaching Initiative
DDA	Disability Discrimination Act
EARLI	European Association for Research on Learning and Instruction
FACT	Formative Automated Computer Testing
FE	further education
HE	higher education
HEFCE	Higher Education Funding Council for England
HEI	Higher Education Institution
HESA	Higher Education Statistics Agency
ICT	Information and Communication Technology
JISC	Joint Information Systems Committee
LTSN	Learning and Teaching Support Network
MCQ	multiple choice question
PASS	Peer Assisted Study Sessions
PDP	Personal Development Plan
PRS	Personal Response System
PSRB	Professional and Statutory Regulatory Body
QAA	Quality Assurance Agency
RTF	Rich Text Format
SEDA	Staff and Educational Development Association
SENDA	Special Education Needs and Discrimination Act
SENLEF	Student Enhanced Learning through Effective Feedback

ABBREVIATIONS

SSR	staff student ratio
TLTP	Teaching and Learning Technology Programme
UKCLE	UK Centre for Legal Education
VLE	Virtual Learning Environment

Introduction

The primary focus of this book is to improve the learning and teaching environment in higher education (HE) by encouraging staff to consider the role of formative assessment and formative feedback and the effect that these have on the student learning experience. The aim is to encourage teaching and support staff to focus on the promotion of student learning through formative assessment activities and the provision of formative feedback (on both formative and summative assessment activities).

One of the major issues for teachers in HE is to get the balance of quality of feedback and timeliness of feedback just right for students in order for students to derive the greatest benefit to their learning from that feedback. There are many challenges facing teachers when they consider the use of formative assessment and formative feedback and many variables to take into account in their practice, ranging from workload issues (for staff and students) to the value placed on the activities and feedback and how these relate to the student learning experience.

Feedback is not unique to higher education and not unique to assessment. We all experience feedback in many different forms whether it is giving or receiving feedback in many different situations in our lives – for example, parenting (talking to our kids), working (appraisals) or coaching (analysing performance and indicating improvements). The skills and techniques employed in these situations have many parallels in the learning environment in higher education.

Providing feedback to students is an important aspect of the teacher's role in higher education. It is suggested in this book that feedback, quality of feedback and timeliness of feedback are key features in the student learning process and in the teacher/student relationship. Feedback is a key aspect in assessment and is fundamental in enabling students to learn from assessment. Helping students to learn from their activities is a key aspect of feedback – particularly through encouraging dialogue. We also need to be aware of the impact that feedback can have in terms of motivation, both intrinsic (wanting to learn) and extrinsic (needing to learn).

Opportunities for teaching staff to give formative feedback to students arise in a wide range of activities and interventions, including informal interactions, classroom situations, one-to-one tutorials, formative assessment activities, online learning, groupwork, as part of the process of summative assessment and work based placements and other work based learning. Each of these activities provide opportunities for formative feedback and can contribute to students' formative development and learning. This brief list also indicates that feedback does not only come from teachers and tutors but also from student peers and work based supervisors and colleagues.

Those involved in teaching in higher education have to balance many expectations and demands on their time, including; teaching, research, subject development, pedagogic development, school roles (for example, programme leading, admissions, placements), university roles, bureau-cracy, quality assurance, professional body expectations and, somewhere in all that mix, personal development!

There are a series of expectations and perceptions of many HE 'stakeholders' for teachers to consider. Stakeholders in assessment (form-ative and summative) include students, academic colleagues, education managers, external examiners, professional bodies and agencies such as the Quality Assurance Agency (QAA). Each stakeholder has a different view on the purpose of assessment activities and a different view on what constitutes appropriate feedback.

Student expectation is a key consideration – and this expectation can be directly affected by the type, and quality, of feedback students encounter. For instance:

- one teacher provides detailed written feedback indicating to students what it is they've done well, how they might improve and resources they may wish to utilise – students then expect the same from all their teachers;
- another teacher provides feedback to all their students (all 250 of them) on a module – students then expect the same turn around on all modules;
- another teacher gives students a series of formative assessment exercises, which the students perceive helps their learning and

understanding – students then expect this type of approach in all their formative activities.

This all takes place in an ever-demanding environment in HE which is set in a context of almost continuous change with increasing student numbers, students with widely ranging abilities and students from different cultures with different educational expectations.

A number of colleagues may be sceptical about the value of formative assessment and formative feedback and that there are other ways students can learn. Some will argue that teachers in HE don't have time or support to be able to provide timely and constructive feedback. Others will argue that students don't want feedback; they just want a numeric mark for work they undertake. Throughout this book these concerns and issues will be addressed and hopefully positive rationale provided as to why feedback is a good thing to be involved in as a teacher and is a good thing for student learning.

This book doesn't suggest that there is a single best solution in formative feedback and formative assessment and certainly not that 'one size fits all'. The aim of the book is to get teachers to think about what it is they are trying to achieve in providing formative assessment activities and providing formative feedback and how these serve to provide an enhanced learning environment for students. In order to achieve this, the intention is to make use of relevant theories and principles to create a pragmatic framework and set of tools that will allow teachers in HE to engage with students through formative activities and dialogue in order to enhance the student learning experience, to guide students in their learning and to encourage students to take responsibility for their own learning.

Many of the principles in formative assessment and formative feedback can be discussed at a generic level, and much of the book is given over to this level of discussion. However, the book incorporates a number of case studies from a range of disciplines outlining the specific challenges and opportunities and expectations in different subject contexts encouraging teachers to:

- think about the purpose of formative assessment and formative feedback when designing student learning activities;
- consider how students engage in formative activities – do they have the appropriate abilities, skills and confidence to participate?

3

- think about whether students will appreciate and value the learning objectives associated with the formative activities – what do they have to do to achieve a successful outcome;
- reflect on their current practice and use of formative feedback (both the formative feedback they give to students and the formative feedback they get from students) to enhance their teaching.

There is nothing more frustrating for teachers after spending hours generating formative feedback when students don't engage in the anticipated learning as a result of the feedback:

- they don't pick up the feedback;
- all they care about is a number;
- they don't know what to do with the feedback when they get it;
- they use the feedback differently from the way the teacher anticipated/expected (this last point is actually an opportunity to engage in dialogue with students and can a) lead to learning opportunities for students through the dialogue and b) help teachers learn about what type of feedback students value in helping their learning).

There are a number of recurring themes which are addressed throughout the book – no apology is made for repetition. In much the same way that students learn from feedback which reinforces a point – so we can learn from having messages reinforced as well. The common themes include:

- involving students in the feedback process – one might think this is fairly obvious, but is actually quite tricky to achieve;
- being clear to students what we are trying to achieve in providing feedback;
- ensuring equity in all formative activities taking into account the diverse student population;
- indicating to students when feedback is taking place;
- explaining to students how formative assessment activities are contributing to their learning;
- providing timely and constructive feedback on assessment activities.

Time Out Sessions

Included in the book are a number of 'time out' sessions. These sessions are not designed to be tests or tasks, but to encourage you to take a step back and think about the points made in the book in the context of your own work.

Example:
▶ What do you want to get from this book?

Chapter 1

Principles of formative assessment and formative feedback

SUMMARY

In this chapter you will be introduced to some of the theoretical and philosophical aspects of formative assessment and formative feedback – discussing the differences between formative assessment and formative feedback. We will outline the role of assessment (summative and formative) in the context of higher education and the culture of assessment in HE, including a discussion on what we are trying to achieve with formative assessment and formative feedback – and by association summative assessment. The chapter will also introduce the suggestion made throughout the book concerning the issue of students currently being driven by summative assessment and how a culture change is required to move to a learner centred environment embracing the principles of formative assessment and feedback.

INTRODUCTION

There is a large amount of literature on assessment – incorporating behaviourist, cognitive, constructivist and sociocultural (situative) approaches to education. Much of the literature on assessment focuses on summative assessment but there is also a large body of literature centred on formative feedback and on formative assessment. Much of the literature, although very valuable, is heavy going for a teacher starting out in higher education. The intention of this book is to utilise the literature in order to deconstruct the theoretical and philosophical aspects of formative feedback and formative assessment and in so doing consider the pragmatics of using formative feedback and formative assessment in your teaching practice in order to enable you to enhance the opportunities for your students to learn.

INITIAL DEFINITIONS

Summative assessment

Any assessment activity which results in a mark or grade which is subsequently used as a judgement on student performance.

Ultimately judgements using summative assessment marks will be used to determine the classification of award at the end of a course or programme.

Formative assessment

Any task or activity which creates feedback (or feedforward) for students about their learning. Formative assessment does not carry a grade which is subsequently used in a summative judgement.

Formative feedback

Formative feedback is any information, process or activity which affords or accelerates student learning based on comments relating to either formative assessment or summative assessment activities.

This chapter deals with some of the theory associated with formative assessment and formative feedback. In order to appreciate the concept of formative assessment and feedback it is important to briefly look at assessment in general. We will consider the underlying principles of assessment before looking at what it might mean for your teaching practice (addressed later in this book). It is a bit tedious, but please stick with it – it will all drop into place later!

Formative assessment and formative feedback are very powerful and potentially constructive learning tools. Very simply, any task that creates feedback (information which helps a student learn from formative activities) or feedforward (information which will help a student amend or enhance activities in the future) to students about their learning achievements can be called formative assessment. All learning and teaching interactions between teacher and student in higher education (and between students and other students) are to some extent formative in nature. Lecturers and tutors need to be aware of the impact of these interactions on student learning and student motivation irrespective of whether the interaction is intended to be formative or not.

For the purposes of this book, formative assessment is defined as any task that creates feedback (or feedforward) to students about their learning. Black and Wiliam (1998) suggest that formative assessment refers to 'all those activities undertaken by teachers (and by their students in assessing themselves), which provide [formative] feedback to shape and develop the teaching and learning activities in which both teachers and students are engaged'.

In this book the suggestion that formative feedback is a 'good thing' is endorsed and that formative assessment can provide opportunities for formative feedback in a supportive, constructive and open environment. It is suggested throughout this book that there is too much emphasis in higher education on summative assessment and that a shift away from the 'testing' and judgement culture associated with summative assessment would alter the learning environment in higher education and provide positive student learning opportunities, encourage dialogue between teachers and students (and between students and students), enhance the student learning experience, provide motivation for students by moving toward a formative assessment ethos and allow students to take responsibility and ownership for their learning and education.

The underpinning principle promoted in this book is that formative assessment and formative feedback should provide positive student learning opportunities, encourage dialogue and discourse between students and teachers, enhance the student learning experience and provide motivation for students. Whether we are able to replace summative assessment by formative assessment (Black and Wiliam, 1998) depends on a number of variables – addressed throughout this book – and it is hoped that by considering these it will help in determining the most appropriate and viable assessment practice depending on the educational environment and circumstance in which the reader is employed.

As indicated in the introduction to the book there are a number of common themes that will be addressed throughout this book, including:

- the involvement and engagement of students in the feedback process – one might think this is fairly obvious, but is actually quite tricky to achieve;
- clarifying for students what teachers are trying to achieve through the provision of feedback – particularly in terms of student learning;
- indicating to students when feedback is taking place – particularly important when providing verbal feedback;
- explaining to students how formative assessment activities are contributing to their learning;

- providing timely and constructive feedback on assessment activities;
- ensuring equity and equality in all formative activities taking into account the diverse student population.

Related to the development of formative assessment and the provision of formative feedback is the aspiration that through improving formative assessment and formative feedback there will be a resultant shift from summative assessment as the focus of learning from both teachers and students. This will be achieved through a reduction in the amount of summative assessment in universities and by encouraging students to engage in formative activities rather than being driven and motivated solely by summative activities. It is hoped that this book will encourage academic staff to consider the balance between formative and summative assessment, and at the same time consider the objectives, purpose, value and amount of summative assessment currently used.

DILEMMA

Teachers in HE would love to provide learning activities and opportunities that encourage students to engage with the curriculum and develop their subject knowledge as well as their personal development. Teachers would love to provide personalised feedback, taking great care over the words used in formative feedback so as to encourage and motivate students and help them develop their knowledge and understanding. Teachers would love to be sensitive to individual students' needs and expectations, culture and disposition. But there is a dilemma – there is currently an environment of mass higher education, there are staff student ratios (SSRs) of 27:1, 35:1 or even 45:1, there is an increasingly diverse student body, there are many teaching pressures on staff, there are all sorts of bureaucratic demands and there is an expectation that staff participate in research. How are formative assessment and formative feedback going to fit into a very full curriculum and a very full schedule? Liu and Carless (2006) indicate that managing time and workloads are significant challenges in the provision of feedback, especially when we seek to increase the quality and regularity of feedback.

There has been in a move in the UK towards mass higher education and as student numbers have increased there have been changes in the nature of higher education and economies of scale in learning and teaching methods – for example, larger classes, reduced contact hours and e-learning.

9

However, some have argued (Gibbs and Simpson, 2004) that the economies of scale have not taken place in assessment. Effectively this means that there is a huge pressure on teachers and students in dealing with the amount of summative assessment. It is suggested in this book that such pressures are to the detriment of the student learning experience. Not only does it mean that students are driven by summative assessment, but that the summative assessment will curb other learning activities such as wider reading, groupwork and formative activities! In addition to this, Glover and Brown (2006) argue that the burden of the amount of summative assessment will mean that feedback is too slow and lacks the necessary quality to be effective (we will return to timeliness of feedback in Chapter 3).

THE STUDENT EXPERIENCE

The concepts of the 'student experience' and the 'student learning experience' are alluded to throughout this book. However, we need to remember that all students will have unique 'student experiences' and unique 'student learning experiences'. The diversity of students across the higher education sector and even the diversity of students in one institution mean that we need to contend with a range of student experiences, a range of student expectations and a range of ways that students learn!

ENHANCEMENT

It is hoped that the book will contribute to the enhancement of teaching practice in the context of formative assessment and formative feedback and by association summative assessment and other teaching and learning activities. As a result of enhancing teaching practice there will be a consequent enhancement in the student learning environment and learning opportunities through changes and improvements in pedagogy.

 Time Out

▶ What opportunities do you have for enhancement in your institution?

▶ What support do you get from your institution, school, mentor in terms of enhancement?

THE PURPOSE OF ASSESSMENT

Colleagues, both those new to higher education and those with a number of years' experience, may well be concerned about assessment and wonder what all the student assessment they set and mark, as part of their work, is actually for! Many will think that the process of summative assessment is actually a judgement on them as academics, judged by students, by peers (internal moderation, exam boards and internal quality review), external examiners and external bodies such as the Quality Assurance Agency or subject specialist professional bodies. They will think of assessment purely in summative terms and not have time to consider formative assessment.

It goes without saying that assessment is important in higher education, particularly as far as students are concerned. Brown (2001) suggests that 'assessment defines what students regard as important, how they spend their time and how they come to see themselves as individuals'. Gibbs and Simpson (2004) suggest that 'assessment is seen to exert a profound influence on student learning: on what students focus their attention on, on how much they study, on their quality of engagement with learning tasks, and, through feedback, on their understanding and future learning'.

If summative assessment 'goes wrong' then it is perceived (by students, teachers and other stakeholders) that there will be some sort of repercussion. As higher education in the UK moves into a new era of fee paying students – many advocating that these students should be considered as customers – it is likely that student appeals will increase if they do not achieve the grades they want (irrespective of the majority of Higher Education Institutions (HEIs) not permitting appeal against academic judgement).

Summative assessment needs to be reliable, valid, affordable and fit for purpose, i.e. usable. Reliability in assessment requires the assessment to be objective, accurate, repeatable and analytically sound, according to Knight (2001). In essence reliability refers to the consistency of grades that are awarded and can be affected by marker consistency, inter-marker reliability and/or test/retest reliability. Validity focuses on the extent to which an assessment measures what it intends to measure and as such contributes to assessing the things programme specifications, programme learning outcomes and module learning outcomes say are important and of value. We will address affordability when considering workloads later in this chapter and usability later in this book.

A review of the literature on assessment suggests a range of functions of summative assessment including:

- The measurement of student ability and understanding as argued for example in Black (1999: 118) who suggests summative assessment 'serves to inform an overall judgement of achievement, which may be needed for reporting and review' – invariably this use of assessment is used in some form of selection process.

- As a means of giving feedback to students – for example Pelligrino *et al*. (2001: 42) suggest that 'an assessment is a tool designed to observe students' behaviour and produce data that can be used to draw reasonable inferences about what students know'.

- To provide feedback to academic staff by using summative assessment as a measurement of the success of learning and teaching, for example Wiliam (2000) suggests that an aspect of summative assessment is to 'provide information with which teachers, educational administrators and politicians can be held accountable to the wider public', an argument supported by Pelligrino *et al*. (2001: 42) suggesting that 'assessments serve a vital role in providing information to help students, parents, teachers, administrators and policy makers to reach decisions'.

- The accountability of academic staff, for example in the argument put forward by Black (1999: 118) that results of assessment 'may also be used for judging the achievement of individual teachers or of schools as a whole'.

- Related to the previous point, a means of monitoring standards, as argued in Wiliam (2000), and the standard can be measured at individual, module, programme, school, institution, sector, national or international levels.

- As a means of enabling student learning during assessment activities (Rowntree, 1987), although Rowntree does suggest that this might be an 'instrument of coercion' getting students to participate in activities that they wouldn't normally choose to take part in.

- As a means of motivating students as suggested by the Assessment Reform Group (1999) – although assessment can provide motivational opportunities for students consideration needs to be given to the potential demotivating impact of assessment.

- Preparation for life (Falchikov, 2005) – traditionally seen as an input to employment or career advancement, but Falchikov argues that more important skills such as collaboration and sharing can be developed through assessment.

All these factors contribute to an inordinate amount of stress on academic staff when dealing with assessment. It is little wonder that people feel pressure when they are engaging in assessment – both staff and students. The range of issues associated with assessment also mean that it is an item which is often under scrutiny from institutional management, school management, external examiners and other external bodies. As we'll see in the 'Problems with Summative Assessment' section measuring the effectiveness of teaching or the quality of teaching by looking at summative assessment results is not necessarily the most appropriate way to make judgements on teaching staff.

Black (1993) suggests that assessment has three broad purposes, namely:

1) the certification of student achievement (normally through summative assessment);
2) the accountability of educational institutions and the education system through the publication and the comparison of results (summative results); and
3) the promotion of learning through the provision of helpful feedback (normally through formative assessment and formative feedback).

Black's second point is a potential issue with summative assessment, or certainly the use of the results of summative assessment, when it is used as a measure of the quality of teaching. Outcomes and performance in summative assessment are only one of the variables that contribute to the quality of teaching and it is difficult to isolate these variables from each other. However, organisations, such as the QAA, use the outputs of summative assessments to make judgements on teaching standards.

This book will focus mainly on how we can apply Black's third point and will attempt to promote the need for formative assessment and formative feedback as part of the process of enabling student learning and enhancing teaching practice. Formative assessment is not simply about setting a series of exercises where students receive feedback. Formative assessment and formative feedback are integral to the student learning process and learning experience and as such they are key aspects of learning and teaching.

13

Time Out

▶ Why do you engage in assessment?

▶ What expectations are placed on you in the context of assessment?

▶ What do you want your students to achieve through assessment?

PROBLEMS WITH SUMMATIVE ASSESSMENT

The literature on assessment indicates that there is a concern regarding the effectiveness of summative assessment. Biggs (1996) suggests that 'testing has not always promoted good learning and indeed can have detrimental effects' and Black and Wiliam (1998), argue that summative assessment is not a particularly good means of finding out what it is that students know.

Falchikov (2005) identifies many of the problems associated with summative assessment:

1) emphasis on examinations
2) issues in reliability and teacher marking bias
3) does not contribute positively to student motivation
4) students play the game – see also Gibbs (2005)
5) doesn't promote deep learning but encourages surface learning
6) contributes to student stress.

Pelligrino (2001: 26–28) suggests the concerns with summative assessment can be summarised as:

1) Concern relating to whether summative assessment 'effectively captures the kind of complex knowledge and skills' with assessments not focusing on the 'many aspects of cognition that research indicates is important'.
2) Usefulness of assessment in improving learning and teaching – summative assessment only provides limited information about

students' understanding and does not provide teachers with an indication of the type of interventions required to improve students' learning.

3) Assessment only providing a snapshot – indicating a measure of student achievement at the time of assessment (although many would contest even this claim) but not providing a measure of student progress or development over a period of time.

4) Concerns regarding fairness and equity – concern regarding potential bias in marking but also concerns about aligning assessment with the material students are taught.

 Time Out

► What causes you the biggest amount of frustration in your summative assessment activities?

► What can you do to address the frustration?

Many Higher Education Institutions moved to a modularised or unitised structure in the 1990s which was supposed to allow for students to accumulate academic credits and move between programmes and institutions in building up enough credit to obtain an award. This process had a significant impact on assessment, particularly on formative assessment and formative feedback – a greater amount of summative assessment and more frequent summative assessment meant less time for formative activities. The notion of holistic programmes and courses which were structured to allow students time to engage in their learning without the pressures of a continuous and heavy summative assessment load disappeared with modularisation.

Many modules or units were designed as small 10- or 15-point 'chunks' all of which had to be assessed and were normally taken over a 12- or 15-week semester – there are of course a number of exceptions to this structure, but it was very common, particularly in post-1992 universities.

One of the consequences of modularisation was that summative assessment had to take place more frequently, often without giving students

15

the time to absorb their learning, experiment or undertake any trial and error learning. A common situation was for students to finish their teaching in one week and be examined on the module the next. Entwhistle and Entwhistle (2003) bring attention to this situation suggesting that students lose the opportunity for revision or consolidating their learning and understanding before examinations. There was (and still is) very little time for formative activities and little time for teachers to provide constructive formative feedback. The consequence of this is that students become driven by summative assessment, disengage with formative assessment and feel that formative feedback on end-of-module summative assessments adds no value to their future modules.

Summative assessment tends to occur towards the end of courses; as suggested by Torrance and Pryor (2002: 8) 'summative assessment is generally considered to be undertaken at the end of a course or programme of study in order to measure and communicate pupil performance and (latterly) accountability'. Brown (1999: 6) supports Torrance and Pryor's suggestion by arguing that summative assessment 'tends to be end point, largely numerical and concerned mainly with making evaluative judgement'. The fact that summative assessment tends to be at the end of a period of study may have an adverse impact on students managing their time effectively or may mean that they have too much summative assessment to deal with at one time.

At the author's institution a move toward larger modules and year-long modules has been implemented, which serves to reduce the amount of summative assessment and allows for formative feedback. However, this type of approach contributes other problems particularly with progression regulations and multiple-point intakes (January starts, for example).

The concerns regarding students being driven by summative assessment will be returned to when considering culture changes (section later in this chapter) and the student learning environment in Chapter 2.

FORMATIVE ASSESSMENT

Yorke (2003: 478) suggests that the basic principle behind formative assessment is to 'contribute to student learning through the provision of information about performance'. Yorke indicates the difficulties in addressing formative assessment by asserting that it is a 'concept that is more complex than it might at first appear'. As indicated in the introduction to this chapter, for the purposes of this book formative assessment can be taken as any task that creates feedback (or feedforward) to students about their learning. Black and Wiliam (1998) suggest that assessment refers to

> all those activities undertaken by teachers (and by their students in assessing themselves), which provide feedback to shape and develop the teaching and learning activities in which both teachers and students are engaged. This becomes 'formative assessment' when the evidence is actually used to adapt the teaching to meet the needs of students or by students themselves to change the way they work at their own learning.

Sadler's (1989: 120) discussion on formative assessment focuses on the concept of using formative assessment to mould students: 'formative assessment is concerned with how judgements about the quality of student responses (performance, pieces, or works) can be used to shape and improve students' competences by short-circuiting the randomness and inefficiency of trial and error learning'. Black and Wiliam (1998: 61) reviewed nearly 700 research publications on formative assessment, and focusing on the most relevant 250 concluded that 'formative assessment does improve student learning'. Torrance and Pryor (2002) support the assertion that formative assessment is positive and can make a considerable difference to the quality of student learning.

Formative assessment is different from summative assessment in what it seeks to achieve. The primary focus of formative assessment (and formative feedback) is to help students understand the level of learning they have achieved and clarify expectations and standards. It is important that formative assessment activities and formative feedback should be aligned to module learning outcomes and where possible indicate where and how they contribute to programme learning outcomes.

In *Inside the Black Box*, Black and Wiliam (1998) claim that their study on formative assessment provides 'firm evidence that indicates clearly a direction for change which could improve standards of learning'; they go on to make a plea that 'national policy will grasp this opportunity and give a lead in this direction'.

Formative assessment is potentially a powerful contributor to student learning in that:

a) Students are more likely to be open about their concerns and weaknesses and enter into dialogue with teachers and/or peers (Black and Wiliam, 1998). According to Knight

17

(2001: 8) 'good formative assessment means design learning sequences that afford plenty of opportunities for good learning conversations arising from feedback on good tasks that are matched to course learning outcomes' – see Chapter 3 for discussion.

b) The stakes are not as high as in summative assessment (students are more likely to experiment and take risks, also means that there is not the same requirement to be so concerned about reliability and validity of assessment tasks) (Knight, 2001).

c) There is the opportunity to enter into dialogue with students about their formative activities and discuss their learning needs (Black, 1999; Black and Wiliam, 1999; Juwah *et al.*, 2004; Hyatt, 2005; Gibbs, 2005).

d) Students can be motivated to learn to enhance their knowledge and understanding rather than to focus on passing summative assessment (Knight, 2001).

e) There is the opportunity to enhance the process of independent learning (Marshall and Rowland, 1998).

f) The formative development of students can contribute to the evidence base in students' Personal Development Plans (PDPs) (Ward, 1999) – see Chapter 3 for details.

g) Students' self-assessment practices and skills can be developed (Black and Wiliam, 1998).

h) Formative assessment can contribute to reflective learning – see Chapter 3 for model and reflective framework.

i) There is the environment to provide an increased opportunity for peer- and self-assessment.

Race (1994) in formulating his 'ripple model' for learning asked numerous academics and students to describe what helped them learn. The majority highlighted practice; trial and error; having a go and experimenting. He noted that to allow learners to make mistakes in a constructive environment is an essential part of learning. Formative assessment is potentially a powerful contributor to this learning process in that students will be more likely to experiment and take risks, as the stakes are not as high as with summative assessment. When carefully managed to include reflection (and / or feedback) as pointed out by Sadler (1989), formative assessment can also be used to resolve these issues.

Close links can also be made with learning models such as Kolb's (1984) model of experiential learning – this concept will be returned to in more detail in Chapter 3 of this book in the section on 'Formative Feedback and Reflective Learning'.

There is a problem with formative assessment in that it is often the case with formative assessment that students fail to recognise formative assessment as a helpful signal (Tunstall and Gipps, 1996), or don't even realise that they are getting formative feedback. It is incumbent on teachers to help students develop the appropriate skills in learning from feedback and at the same time provide feedback which is well structured, helpful and constructive to motivate students.

DIFFERENCES BETWEEN SUMMATIVE AND FORMATIVE ASSESSMENT

There is an inextricable link between feedback and assessment and herein lies one of the greatest challenges in being able to produce a clear definition between formative and summative assessment. Yorke (2003) refers to this 'definitional fuzziness' being due to the range of formative assessment: from a very informal process where feedback is likely to be verbal through to tasks which are actually intended to functionally perform in a formative manner but in reality act summatively, for example written feedback (formative) on a student assignment (summative). Hence, this can result in an academic misconception over original formative purpose and/or lead to confusion on the part of the student as to the intentional role of the feedback as something to be acted upon as opposed to judging performance.

The differences between summative and formative assessment are summarised very effectively in Knight (2001: 3–11), which can be accessed at the HE Academy website at www.heacademy.ac.uk/.

Appreciating the differences between summative and formative assessment can potentially be confusing especially for new lecturers as they begin to become exposed to educational jargon. A straightforward definition of the difference between the two is provided in Knight (2001) indicating that summative assessment is for 'judgement' and formative assessment for 'improvement'. However, this is where Yorke's argument of 'it's not as simple as it seems' comes into play.

The potential confusion becomes apparent when formative feedback is given on summative assessment or summative marks are allocated to formative activities – see section later in this chapter. The author argues that the first scenario is a positive way to use assessment for learning, but does not advocate the second scenario – however, many practitioners use this approach in order to encourage student participation in formative activities – see Chapter 2 for more detail.

Gibbs (2005) suggests 'feedback' should still be associated with summative assessment, with formative assessment allied with 'feedforward'. Knight (2001) characterises 'feedback' as the product of formative assessment, with summative assessment resulting in 'feedout'. It should be emphasised that this terminology is not yet commonplace, although the author subscribes to Gibbs' distinction between feedback and feedforward. If feedforward is to be used effectively there need to be links between modules and a more holistic curriculum (certainly a more holistic curriculum than that normally offered under modularisation). It also needs students to appreciate the value of feedforward and be provided with clear transparent rationale to encourage them to learn from the feedforward.

In summative assessment the stakes are high (for students, academics, and the university) whereas formative assessment allows for greater risk taking, experimentation, discussion and development. In formative assessment there is not the same level of requirement to ensure assessment reliability or validity, although assessment concepts such as affordability and usability do need to be considered.

Reducing the stakes in assessment by moving towards a culture of formative assessment may well lead to some of the pressure being removed from students (assuming the students engage with the formative activities – see discussion in Chapter 2). When the assessment pressure is removed – predominantly taking away the notion of marks, scores or grades – then the opportunity to design formative assessment activities to encourage learning and formative development can be incorporated.

Making use of formative activities to facilitate student learning will allow students to:

1) think about what it is they are trying to learn;
2) try things out and learn from mistakes (as an aside, this was how the author learned to programme computers);
3) think about what it is they want to learn;
4) discuss subjects they don't understand;
5) take into account the possibility of different interpretation of the formative assessment activities; and
6) consider and reflect on their learning needs.

(See also the discussion on assessment for learning later in this chapter.)

20

Should the balance between formative and summative assessment change between levels?

George and Cowan (1999) indicate that in the early stages of student learning the emphasis should be on formative assessment rather than summative, with the balance changing as students get closer to the award stage, with the emphasis moving towards summative.

The author has attempted to put in place an assessment strategy in his own institution which would move away from summative assessment altogether at level 4 (first year) with the whole year being formative – suggesting a 120-point module which would be mainly diagnostic – the suggestion met with more than a little resistance from colleagues (outright hostility if the truth be told – see later in this chapter for discussion on managing change in higher education). However at Abertay University a novel approach to level 4 assessment has been implemented on one of their programmes where students develop a portfolio over the year across all their subjects and are then vivaed at the end of the year – giving a summative hurdle to a formative activity.

FORMATIVE FEEDBACK

There is a close relationship between formative assessment and formative feedback (although feedback can occur on summative assessment). Wiliam and Black (1996) identify feedback as a key component of formative assessment. Black and Wiliam (1999) suggest a definition of formative assessment which includes the importance of feedback, which is 'any teacher assessment which diagnoses students' difficulties and provides constructive feedback leads to significant learning gains'.

The rationale for considering feedback in the context of higher educa-tion is that appropriate use of feedback can enhance student learning. If we assume that providing opportunities for learning is the key function of higher education then interventions, such as feedback, contribute to student learning. Pellegrino *et al.* (2001: 234) suggest that 'learning is a process of continuously modifying knowledge and skills' and that feedback is essential to 'guide, test challenge or redirect the learner's thinking'. Stefani (1998) argues that supportive feedback, both oral and written, when it is given in a supportive and constructive way is a vital element for student learning.

Hounsell (2004) defines formative feedback as 'any information, process or activity which affords or accelerates learning, whether enabling students to achieve higher quality learning outcomes than they might otherwise

21

have attained, or by enabling them to attain these outcomes more rapidly'. Hattie (1987) undertaking a meta-analysis of what makes a difference to student achievement indicates that the most powerful influence is feedback.

In the QAA Code of Practice on Assessment (2000) it is stated that it is incumbent on HE institutions to 'ensure that appropriate feedback is provided to students on assessed working in a way that promotes learning and facilitates improvement'. If it is assumed that formative assessment and formative feedback are important and 'good' things then there is a need to examine how formative assessment and feedback can be used effectively to enhance teaching and promote student learning.

 Time Out

▶ What type of feedback do you provide for your students?

▶ When do you provide this feedback?

▶ What steps do you take to ensure your feedback has a formative function?

▶ In what ways do you hope your feedback contributes to your students' learning? (Will they learn? Will they remember?)

▶ Do you know how students use your feedback?

Black (1999) suggests the following as the basic principles of formative feedback:

- goals (learning objectives) need to be clear to students;
- feedback should measure (give guidance to) the student's current learning state;
- formative feedback should be used as a means for closing the gap between the student's learning state and the learning goals;
- formative feedback needs to be high quality and effective in its advice.

Throughout this book these principles are considered and developed in the context of the implications for your teaching practice.

22

Formative feedback is closely linked to formative assessment but it can also potentially be used as a link between summative assessment and formative development.

Formative feedback is normally provided by teachers or tutors but can also take the form of feedback provided through peer-assessment or be part of a self-assessment or a personal reflective exercise. Black (1999: 118) continues with this thread indicating that formative assessment is 'concerned with the short term collection and use of evidence for the guidance of learning, mainly in day to day classroom practice'.

Brown *et al.* (1997) report that the effects of student feedback are one of the 'better tested principles in psychology'. Sadler (1989) noted that feedback is the 'key element' in formative assessment but stated that feedback can only serve a formative function when it (feedback) is used to alter the gap between current and the required/expected levels of understanding, an element under student control.

Formative feedback should endeavour to provide students with an indication of where they are in relation to achieving learning outcomes or standards, where they need to progress to and how they will be able to reach the expected level. In order for this to be effective the feedback should be based on understood goals (for the student) which the student believes are achievable and valuable. Feedback should be understandable and communicated in such a way as to enable students to use the feedback to help in achieving the learning outcomes or reaching the required standard. Similarly feedback should be worded in such a way as to encourage students to take actions to address any learning issues.

FORMATIVE FEEDBACK ON SUMMATIVE ASSESSMENT

It has already been suggested in this chapter that there is a certain fuzziness as to the distinction between formative and summative activities. Providing formative feedback on summative assessments is one of the main reasons for confusion as to what is formative and what is summative. It is often the case that summative assessments are designed to encourage students to learn and also to provide formative feedback from teachers.

When formative feedback is included as feedback on summative assessments it can help the process of learning from the assessment. However in order to be valuable, and perceived by students to be valuable, feedback needs to be relevant to future assessments and to the student

23

learning process. The relevance of feedback for future learning can be enhanced by:

- ensuring holistic curriculum – and that students understand how various bits of programmes join together;
- providing feedback that will address future issues – feedforward – as well as providing feedback on the summative work submitted;
- encouraging students to develop deep learning.

Nicol and Macfarlane-Dick (2004: 11) suggest that a great deal of 'feedback information is often about strengths and weaknesses of handed-in work or about aspects of performance that are easy to identify (such as spelling mistakes) rather than about aspects that are of greater importance to academic learning but that are more abstract and difficult to define (such as strength of argument)'.

Providing feedback on summative assessments allows teachers the opportunity to contextualise the feedback based on the student work and indicate where students have done well, where there might be issues, where they can 'close the gap' and what developmental activities to feedforward to future assessments or modules. There is debate in the literature as to what type of feedback students want (returned to in Chapter 2). There is a suggestion – for example Adams *et al.* (2000) – that students only want numeric marks as a form of recognition.

The issues discussed earlier in this chapter regarding modularisation have an impact on formative feedback on summative assessment. If summative assessment takes place at the end of the module there are potential problems in timing and perceived student value of the feedback. Even if a summative assessment takes place within a module there are serious time constraints in getting the feedback to the students before their next summative assessment.

The issues in timeliness of feedback can be exacerbated by the need for the summative assessment process to be robust, reliable and valid. Taking into account the need to assure the summative assessment through means such as double-marking, blind double-marking and moderation, while assuring the assessment measurement also has the effect of slowing the process down.

The discussion in this section has focused on formative feedback on coursework as summative assessment. Examinations are of course a significant type of summative assessment and a number of professional bodies expect a large proportion of summative assessment to be undertaken

24

through examination. Examinations are often seen as an assessment instrument that addresses the problem of plagiarism. It has already been indicated in this chapter that examinations are not necessarily the most effective assessment instrument; there are issues about what examinations actually measure and examinations are not necessarily constructive in encouraging student learning. In terms of formative feedback exams tend to be at the end of modules and often university regulations prohibit formative learning opportunities through feedback on examination papers.

THE CASE AGAINST FEEDBACK

As identified in the introduction to this book and elsewhere in Chapter 1 the provision of good quality feedback which will enhance student learning is not an easy thing to do. It is not always the case that students benefit from feedback or indeed learn anything from feedback. This is particularly frustrating when time and effort and best intentions have been put into providing feedback. Swing (2004) suggests that 'not all students desire feedback from their teachers, the myth of the eager learner breathlessly awaiting wise feedback from their professors endures'.

Discussion on the way students use feedback, what they learn from feedback and what they expect from feedback will be returned to in more detail in Chapter 2. Outlined below are some of the problems associated with feedback (further examples of good and not so good practice are addressed in Chapter 4):

1) Students don't make use of the feedback (Hounsell, 1987) – they are interested only in grades or marks.
2) Feedback doesn't actually contribute to student learning – especially when feedback is not constructive, isn't understood by students (Lea and Street, 1998), is too complex or is contradictory.
3) Feedback is only there to justify the mark that students are given (MacLellan, 2001).
4) Feedback may be categorical in tone and not particularly explicit (Mutch, 2003).
5) There isn't an opportunity for students to enter into dialogue or discourse about their feedback.
6) Feedback emphasises the power relationship between teachers and students – especially if the teacher is providing all the

25

feedback without opportunity for dialogue between teacher and students.

7) Provision of feedback has the potential to include bias – it is difficult to ensure that feedback is fair. One of the main concerns from students is that they want feedback to be fair (Holmes and Smith, 2003).

8) Feedback may actually foster rote learning – especially as a reaction to frequent feedback.

9) Feedback might actually be inappropriate – for example giving positive feedback to make students feel better or encourage students irrespective of the quality of the work being assessed (Pelligrino *et al.*, 2001).

WORKLOAD ISSUES

As well as considering how teachers can improve feedback by addressing issues such as timeliness, extent of feedback and quality of feedback, a great deal of the literature on feedback is given over to how to manage the process of generating feedback so that the teacher's workload is not dominated by creating feedback.

It is recognised that significant effort is required in the design of effective formative assessment activities and the production of quality formative feedback. Hence, there is a need for commitment, engagement and 'buy in' from all those concerned, i.e. management, academic staff, administrative support and, perhaps most importantly, students.

As well as an educational and motivational rationale for the reduction in summative assessment and the improvement of formative assessment there is a pragmatic workload consideration to take into account. If summative and formative activities exist in parallel there is the potential that an intolerable burden will be placed on academic members of staff and students.

 Time Out

▶ Early in this chapter the notion of timely feedback has been addressed as has the concept of constructive high quality feedback.

▶ What does this mean for your workload?

There are some strategies for reducing the workload and expectation on staff, for example:

1) Reducing the overall amount of summative assessment will free up time to spend on constructive formative activities.
2) Running formative and summative activities in parallel (Wiliam and Black,1996).
3) Utilising opportunities for peer- and self-assessment in formative activities, including giving formative feedback – peer- and self-assessment will be returned to in Chapter 4.

ASSESSMENT FOR LEARNING

The reduced emphasis on summative assessment promoted in this book aligns with the primary focus with the assessment for learning as defined by Northumbria University's Centre for Excellence in Teaching and Learning (CETL). McDowell *et al.* (2005) identify six conditions of Assessment for Learning (AfL) supported by learning environments that:

1) emphasise authenticity and complexity in the content and methods of assessment rather than the reproduction of knowledge and reductive assessment;
2) use high-stakes summative assessment rigorously but sparingly rather than as the main driver for learning;
3) offer students extensive opportunities to engage in the kinds of tasks that develop and demonstrate their learning, thus building their confidence and capabilities before they are summatively assessed;
4) are rich in feedback derived from formal mechanisms;
5) are rich in informal feedback ideally providing a continuous flow on 'how they are doing';
6) develop students' abilities to direct own learning, evaluate their own progress and attainments and support the learning of others.

There is a recognition in Assessment for Learning that summative assessment has its appropriate place. However, within AfL framework four of the six conditions primarily shift focus toward formative activity. The emphasis in AfL is to design assessment activities which encourage students to learn from assessment. Formative assessment is a 'safer' way for students to take risks and try things out in their learning.

CULTURE CHANGE IN ASSESSMENT

One of the themes in the remainder of this book is to shift the emphasis from summative assessment to formative assessment and to allow students the opportunity to learn from their assessment activities rather than be driven by completing summative assessments. This argument has been put forward earlier in the chapter, particularly with reference to level 4 (first year degree) but is relevant to all levels of study in HE. The Assessment for Learning CETL also advocates a move from summative to formative assessment.

In any change in education it is important to consider the impact on the people who will need to work with the changes, in order for that change to be successful. Morrison (1998: 17) stresses the point, 'change is likely to be successful if it is: congruent with existing practices in the school; understood and communicated effectively; triallable and trialled; seen to be an improvement on existing practice by the participants; seen to further the direction in which the institution is moving'. If formative activities are to replace summative assessment as the predominant assessment mechanism then the benefits to students to staff and to other stakeholders need to be clear. It is hoped that this book will contribute to a culture change in the nature of assessment.

Morrison (1998: 13) suggests that change is a 'process of transformation, either initiated by internal factors or external forces, involving individuals, groups or institutions, leading to a realignment of existing values, practices and outcomes'. In proposing changes in assessment we need to consider where the changes are coming from and who the changes are for.

As Gibbs (2005) has indicated there is an overwhelming burden of summative assessment on students and staff – to the detriment of learning. Any change should be seen to reduce the workload burden. The other main benefit in change is to improve the student learning opportunities. It has been argued elsewhere in this chapter that formative activities have the potential to encourage and enhance student learning and as such students will benefit.

From a management perspective there is a huge cost associated with assessment. It has been suggested for example (Gibbs, 2005) that the cost of assessment is now greater than the cost of teaching in HEIs in the UK. It would therefore seem timely to address the volume of assessment from the financial perspective as well as the educational one.

If students encounter an improved learning experience then it should be the case that other stakeholders benefit, but, again going back to Yorke

(2003) it is not always as simple as that. Management in HEIs and external stakeholders – such as the QAA, professional bodies and employers – may well take a different view of a change in the levels of summative assessment. Fullan's (1991: 106) view that 'conflict and disagreement are not only inevitable but fundamental to successful change' will no doubt be applied to the summative/formative debate.

There are many reasons for not wanting to change the culture of assessment, including:

1) teachers in HE not being convinced by the arguments for change;
2) change imposed without consultation or participation;
3) students not wanting to change their approach to assessment;
4) lack of incentive to change;
5) resistance to change;
6) effort required to change – change in practice, change in documentation, change in regulations;
7) institutional inertia – not allowing change to take place.

It is therefore incumbent on you to contribute to the change process, generating a bottom-up critical mass – hopefully the remainder of this book will convince you of the benefits of formative assessment and formative feedback.

SUMMARY

Assessment is a major issue in higher education – an inordinate amount of emphasis is placed on assessment (particularly summative assessment) and a huge amount of time and effort goes into delivering, managing and assuring assessment. Assessment is stressful for students and for staff. Assessment has many functions in HE – but much of the focus is on summative assessment and within summative assessment the focus is on using the assessment as an instrument to measure student ability and understanding. Summative assessment has to be reliable and valid and this adds to the complexity around assessment and has the potential to make assessment cumbersome and slow.

Shifting the emphasis from summative assessment to formative assessment is not a panacea for all the assessment issues in HE but can contribute to alleviating some of the stresses, pressures and problems. It is suggested in this book that formative assessment and formative feedback can enhance student learning and can be used to motivate students to undertake assessment for learning.

In order for the shift from summative to formative to take place a culture change is required in HE, from the institutional perspective but also from the perspectives of academics and of students.

Chapter 2

Student learning environment

CHAPTER SUMMARY

This chapter examines the learning environment in which students undertake their learning activities to help teachers develop appropriate formative assessment and provide effective formative feedback. It is important to consider the learning environment in higher education from a student perspective. Often the expectations of students and teachers are very different – even when using the same activity as a starting point. It is often the case that the activities that are valued by students are not the same activities that are valued by academics or are not the activities that teachers expect students to value.

This chapter will discuss the motivations and drivers for learning and assessment from a student perspective, with particular reference to participation in formative activities. As well as the academic development of students we need to remember that there are a number of conflicting demands on students' time and effort such as dealing with financial pressures (the need to work), social development, family responsibilities, time management and participation in other activities such as sport and recreation.

The chapter will introduce techniques aimed at encouraging students to participate in formative activities and look at ways that formative assessment and formative feedback can be used to motivate students through encouraging students to value the activities and consider how the activities will enhance their experience of higher education.

INTRODUCTION

In order to develop appropriate formative activities there is a need to appreciate the learning environment in which students work, what motivates students and what type of learning activities students will value.

It is suggested in this chapter (again) that we should be shifting the emphasis from summative assessment to formative assessment and examining how students are motivated to learn. This chapter aims to address student motivation by considering what techniques can be used to improve formative feedback while at the same time getting students to take responsibility for their academic work. By reducing the volume of summative assessment, and by introducing more exciting, interesting, engaging, innovative and valued means of assessment (formative assessment helps remove some of the pressures and stresses) it is hoped the motivation for students to learn can be explored.

As always there is the associated issue of academic workload and the impact that the production of timely and quality feedback will have on teachers. If we assume that assessment is important to student learning and it is important in higher education then it should be resourced appropriately and not seen as an add-on which is done for free. It is not the purpose of this book to discuss the issues surrounding management of higher education but it is important that there is a recognition that to provide constructive formative assessment and feedback takes time and effort. There is an opportunity to address the demands on academics by reducing the amount of summative assessment and replacing it with formative assessment. Other techniques such as peer- and self-assessment (see Chapter 4), Information and Communication Technologies (ICTs) (see Chapter 5), selective assessment and group discussion can be utilised as productive learning techniques which also (potentially) reduce workload.

Yorke (2003) raises a salient question asking whether feedback will lead to change in student behaviour. This theme can be expanded to consider whether feedback will have any impact on student learning. It is hoped that constructive feedback will indeed help students to change their behaviour so that their learning will be enhanced and it is suggested in this chapter that feedback – as well as engagement in formative assessment – will also improve student learning. We do need however to understand assessment and feedback from a student perspective as well as from an academic perspective. Students and teachers often have different perceptions and expectations regarding academic activities, and formative assessment and formative feedback are no exceptions.

HIGHER EDUCATION ENVIRONMENT

At the end of the day, in the UK, we continue to give students classifications (even a pass/fail decision requires a summative judgement) on their awards and as such we continue to depend on summative assessment for purposes of academic judgement. This is not to contradict the arguments in Chapter 1 suggesting a move towards a more formative assessment model; it is an indication of the current requirements and expectations in the higher education environment.

Ramsden (1998: 14) suggests that the HE environment is undergoing a 'fundamental change from an elite system of higher education, largely confined within national boundaries, to a mass higher education system in a global business. Numbers, finance, structure, purposes, students, governance, confines, technologies, the amount of available knowledge and its diversity have all changed'. Although Ramsden was writing in 1998 the environment of change continues to be a significant factor in HE today – for example, the Bologna Declaration (1999) (see HEFCE, 1999) will ensure a continuing environment of change. Much of the change is chaotic and often contradictory – for example, making higher education accessible to everyone and at the same time introducing rises in student fees.

Government policy has a target to increase participation in higher education to 50 per cent of 18–30-year-olds by 2010. Higher Education Statistics Agency (HESA) statistics indicate a 28 per cent rise in the undergraduate student population in the UK between 1996/97 and 2004/05. Students continue to be recruited to universities on merit but from an increasingly diverse variety of academic backgrounds, thus resulting in large groups of mixed ability and diverse learning experiences. Teaching large numbers of mixed ability students presents a significant problem in terms of assessment and the provision of feedback.

There are a huge number of changes currently taking place in higher education – so why should assessment be immune from change? A straightforward answer is that it shouldn't be immune from change and we should be designing assessments which are manageable from a workload point of view, robust (valid and reliable) from an academic quality point of view and effective as learning mechanisms for students. However, as Gibbs (2005) suggests we have not changed our assessment practices, we have not reduced summative assessment and we have not taken into account the increase in student numbers. As a result assessment takes up a proportionately larger amount of time and cost than it ever did before.

STUDENTS IN HIGHER EDUCATION – READING FOR A DEGREE?

The message of one particular lecture delivered by an eminent professor at Edinburgh University has stayed with me long after my undergraduate days (over 20 years ago). He suggested that it didn't matter what he told us as students, indeed he expected us to challenge, question and even disregard much of what he said in his lectures and that it was our duty as students to read for our degrees and take responsibility for our learning. Twenty years on it seems to be a very different environment for learning. It is certain that the traditional approach to reading for a degree still exists in many institutions but there are also many Higher Education Institutions where it does not.

Differences in secondary school education and the diverse routes and qualifications students use as entry to university mean that the academic skills of students cover a multitude of abilities and expectations. When this is coupled with cultural changes and the expectation that reward should be given without necessarily applying a traditional work ethic, then a percentage of students do not seem to expect to have to work independently for, and certainly not read for, their degrees.

This is not to denigrate today's students – not at all. All students in HE have a serious work/life balancing act to manage. As well as a full curriculum, many students have a series of potentially conflicting demands on their time and effort such as holding down part-time (or near permanent) jobs in order to finance their way through university. Many students also have family commitments which have a major impact on the amount of time they can devote to their studies. On top of this, the number of personal problems students have to deal with in today's HE environment means that a smooth passage through their studies is increasingly fraught with difficulties.

Over a period of time the norm of using examinations as the primary instrument of summative assessment has moved to a mix of in-course assessment and examination, with many modules now being assessed by both coursework (multiple courseworks) and examination. When this is combined with the structural issues (alluded to in Chapter 1) as a consequence of modularisation the summative assessment load has continued to expand. As the assessment load has increased, students are driven not by learning or education but by assessment. As students become more driven by assessment then in order to balance their work/life balance they tend to become more strategic and selective in the activities they engage with and the value they attribute to formative activities and the consequent motivation to engage in formative activities is diminished.

Time Out

▶ What do you remember from your time as a student at University?

▶ What assessment types do you remember from University?

▶ What actual assessments (if any) have stuck in your mind?

▶ What type of feedback did you get?

▶ What did you do with the feedback?

▶ Has your University experience shaped the way you now teach?

STUDENT MOTIVATIONS AND DRIVERS

Students in higher education have a wide range of motivations and a variety of drivers. In order for students to learn effectively they need to be motivated to learn. It is not the intention in this book to analyse the various motivational theories. For readers interested in understanding student motivation in more detail, Brown *et al.*'s (1998) text *Motivating Students* is a good starting point. If formative assessment and formative feedback are to be successful learning tools then there is a need to appreciate that formative assessment doesn't solely depend on the learning activity and the resultant feedback, but as Black (1999: 125) suggests 'on the broader context about the motivations and self-perceptions of students'.

In considering motivation as one of the challenges in formative assessment and feedback, we need to appreciate that motivation is not a straightforward subject to understand or to address. Motivation is an intangible concept and will vary between students in a group and between different groups of students. How many times in your experience has a formative exercise worked really well and you repeat the session with a different group of students and it falls completely flat? In addition a student's own motivation will develop and change throughout their time at university – for example, the motivation of a level 4 student during their first semester is likely to be different to a level 6 student completing their final year project. Teachers need to take into account the fact that motivation will change.

Motivation for students to participate and engage in higher education covers a number of drivers, but one of the main motivations associated

35

with learning focuses on forming goals and making an effort to achieve them (related to student ownership of their learning). Race (1995) refers to this as a student's level of 'wanting to learn'.

Students will want to learn for a number of different reasons. The literature on motivation suggests that there are four different (but related) motivational categories:

- *extrinsic motivation* – normally associated with external drivers such as the prospect of employment and the end of a programme of study;
- *intrinsic motivation* – based around the student's desire to learn about their chosen subject;
- *competitive motivation* – performance in assessments often in competition or relation to peers; and
- *social motivation* – desire to succeed in order to please other people such as family members.

It is unlikely that students would be motivated in only one of these ways – it is more likely that there will be a complex mix from all categories. However, we should be aware that students will place different levels of importance (between each other and over time) on each category.

At first glance it may seem that students are driven mainly by extrinsic factors, normally a desire to get a job at the end of their degree, but as we shall see later in the chapter when considering what it is that students expect from feedback, there is evidence of a desire to learn. Feedback can help in addressing intrinsic motivation through encouraging students to learn and to 'close the gap' on their understanding of subjects.

It is suggested in the literature (for example Murphy, 2005) that it is assessment that indicates to students what really matters on a module or programme of study and it is assessment that informs students about the goals of the module or programme. Brown *et al.* (2006) put forward the argument that 'assessment defines what students regard as important, how they spend their time and how they come to see themselves as students and graduates'. Hamdorf and Hall (2001) indicate that assessment is important because it has such a powerful influence on the learning behaviour of students. Assessment can be seen to be one of the key motivators for students and is fundamental in determining what it is that students value in their education.

The effort that students make towards achieving goals is affected by how they feel about those goals and how they perceive the likelihood of achieving those goals. Brown *et al.* (1997) argue that 'students take their cues from what is assessed rather than from what lecturers assert is important'. Assessment can be seen to act as a positive motivator for students if they think the assessment is relevant to their broader goals.

The section on motivation focused on assessment in general and no distinction has been made between summative and formative assessment. The rationale for discussing assessment generally is that because of the amount of summative assessment it is difficult enough to encourage students to participate in summative activities (extrinsic motivation – where they at least see the motivating value of it contributing toward their award) – as opposed to encouraging them to engage in formative activities which are designed to help students understand their subjects (intrinsic motivation). However, the concept of summative assessment being a student driver and students participating and engaging in activities that they perceive as valuable, has an impact on the way we utilise formative activities and the level to which students will engage in formative assessment and formative feedback.

There are a number of areas in which we need to consider motivation, including the motivation to participate in formative activities and the motivation to engage with and learn from feedback (see sections later in this chapter).

It is important that teachers appreciate the motivating effect of feedback, particularly positive feedback, on students. Schunk (1989) suggests that positive feedback will enhance student confidence in their academic abilities and as such improve academic performance as students develop confidence in their academic abilities. In other words a self-perpetuating confidence spiral improves academic performance.

Feedback can have a very positive motivating effect on students, but we need to take great care in ensuring that positive statements are actually helpful. If students are given positive comments purely to encourage and motivate them to engage in further study, or as a reward for the effort they have put in (there is an argument that effort rather than achievement should be rewarded) then they could get a false sense of achievement and false sense of their understanding of the subject.

Not only do we need to take great care in the positive comments we provide for students in our feedback, we need to be careful not to demotivate them. There persists a student belief that teachers 'know best' and so they will react to every comment teachers make. As we shall see later the quality of feedback is not always constructive or 'good' and in Chapter 4 we will see that there are any number of examples of 'bad practice' in the provision of feedback.

37

Students can be demotivated as a result of feedback particularly when:

- they perceive the feedback to be unfair
- feedback is unclear
- they don't understand the feedback
- the feedback doesn't seem to relate to the work they have done
- they don't receive feedback in time
- feedback is overly critical, or
- feedback is non-constructive.

The provision of feedback is a tricky balancing act. When we provide feedback we need to be clear what it is we are providing feedback on. Students are often confused because they are not sure what it is that teachers are giving them feedback about. There are a number of areas in which we can provide feedback including:

- criteria
- subject understanding
- alignment to learning outcomes
- communication skills
- academic skills
- style and approach
- transferable skills
- student effort.

It is suggested in much of the literature on formative feedback that when providing formative feedback, no matter the quality of the work, the formative feedback given to students always opens with a positive and constructive comment. However, other commentators argue against a positive comment followed by a list of criticisms and argue instead for providing students with feedback information mapped against a set of clearly defined criteria.

In another book in this Key Guides Series, Haines (2004) suggests that there are two types of framework for providing feedback:

1) The feedback sandwich – this has three features:
   - first strengths are identified (praise)

- weaknesses (development needs) are identified
- options for improvement are explored — ending on a positive note.

2) The interactive approach — aimed at encouraging self-assessment and reflection:
- ask what the student thinks went well
- say what you (and/or other students) think went well
- ask what could be improved
- say what you (and/or other students) think could be improved
- discuss how the improvements could be brought about.

In addition it is suggested here that the most constructive, and effective, feedback is based on what it is that students want. How do you know what they want? — ask them! What happens when you ask them? — you enter a dialogue! By entering into a dialogue with students about feedback even before we generate the feedback, then the principle of using feedback as a basis for discussion is set. It is through the technique of engaging in dialogue with students about feedback that feedback can really be used to enhance student learning.

 Time Out

▶ Consider how you might engage students in determining the type of feedback that they want you (or their peers) to provide for them.

▶ Do they want a numeric mark? You might discuss why this is not necessarily helpful if they do want this.

▶ Do they want you to identify perceived weaknesses and how to address these weaknesses?

▶ Do they want you to concentrate on one or two points — weaknesses or issues that they might have identified (requires a certain level of skill in self-assessment)?

▶ Do they want you to consider their future learning requirements?

▶ Do they want to discuss the feedback with you?

The quality of feedback and the quality of the feedback experience combined with the perceived value students place on the feedback will influence the probability of students engaging in future formative assessment activities. What is important in formative assessment activities is the quality of student learning as a result of the activity – this does not necessarily mean lots of extra marking for teachers, but does mean that students should be encouraged to engage in the formative activity.

STUDENT EXPECTATIONS

Student expectation is a key consideration – and this expectation can be directly affected by the type, and quality, of feedback students encounter. For example:

- One teacher provides detailed written feedback indicating to students what it is they've done well, how they might improve and resources they may wish to utilise – students then expect the same from all their teachers.
- Another teacher provides quick feedback to all their students (all 250 of them) on a module – students then expect the same turn around on all modules.
- Another teacher gives students a series of formative assessment exercises which the students perceive help their learning and understanding – students then expect this type of approach in all their formative activities.

When student expectations are taken into account, a problem in the consistency of the quality of formative activities and in the consistency of approach in both the use of formative assessment and the nature of the formative feedback may become apparent. In order to tackle the consistency issues it can be helpful to define standards and threshold levels for formative feedback to ensure consistency of approach and equity and equality of the student learning experience across a programme of study or perhaps even at institutional level. Defining standards at institutional levels (except at the most generic of levels) becomes tricky given the differences between subjects and the different feedback requirements of different subjects. Standards and equivalence are particularly important when there are several markers/assessors/teachers on the same module. Students do compare their feedback and their experiences and it is important that we ensure consistency and fairness.

ENCOURAGING STUDENT PARTICIPATION IN FORMATIVE ACTIVITIES

In Chapter 1 we briefly discussed the issue of students participating or indeed not participating in formative activities – engaging with formative assessment activities or making use of formative feedback in their learning. In order to get students to participate in formative activities they need to be motivated to engage – and in order to get them to engage in the formative activities they need to value the activities.

Students don't necessarily engage in activities the way teachers expect them to and will act in situations according to the way they see or value the situation. It is often the case that the activities that are of value to students are not the same things that are of value to academics. This certainly applies in formative assessment and feedback. For example (apologies for generalising and stereotyping) we see formative assessment as a developmental activity and an opportunity to try things out without pressure – students see formative assessment as a valueless activity. We see formative feedback as a time consuming but valuable learning opportunity – students see feedback as criticism.

There is a possibility (maybe even a danger) that students will only engage in assessment activities that have a summative purpose. There are a number of potential reasons for this, including:

a)   it is summative marks that students are judged on/classified on;
b)   academics value summative assessment;
c)   external stakeholders (e.g. employers/parents) value summative assessment results;
d)   there is so much summative assessment that students don't have time for anything else.

If students only focus on summative assessment it potentially means that they will not engage in formative activities because they don't:

a)   appreciate the value of the formative activity as a learning opportunity;
b)   want to spend time on activities that they don't get a 'reward' for;
c)   see the value or relevance of summative assessment activities and as a result believe there is even less value in formative assessment;
d)   see feedback as a positive signal (Black, 1999);

  e) focus on their learning or skills development outside the specific summative expectations of a particular module;

  f) view their educational or professional development as part of their student experience.

All of the above can be summarised as students having a negative attitude towards their learning – and it is addressing this negative view which is one of our main challenges in promoting formative activities, and indeed one of our main challenges in higher education.

When we design formative activities and when we create formative feedback we need to make sure that students value the process and have time to engage in the process. Nicol and Macfarlane-Dick (2004: 3) suggest that formative assessment and feedback should be 'used to empower students as self-regulated learners and that more recognitions should be given to the role of feedback on learners' motivational beliefs and self-esteem'. If we use the rationale of empowerment and encourage students in the direction of wanting to learn then the value of formative activities and the value of participating in those activities should become apparent.

 Time Out

▶ Do you think it is too idealistic to want your students to learn for the sake – or even joy – of learning and to want to develop their knowledge and understanding about subjects?

▶ How do you know your students are engaging in formative activities?

▶ The following are some strategies and techniques you might like to try:

 ■ Review the formative activity.

 ■ Ask your students why they engaged or why they chose not to.

 ■ Work with them to encourage participation – emphasising the benefits.

 ■ Try to find out what it is that they value (this will vary between students).

 ■ Discuss with students the type of feedback that they feel helps them.

 ■ Talk to your students about learning.

 ■ Encourage your students to take responsibility and ownership of their learning.

▶ The process of discourse and dialogue will help in encouraging and motivating students as well as promote formative activities and enhance learning.

Some practitioners make use of summative reward for engaging in formative assessment. The rationale often given is that it will encourage student participation in formative activities. However, it is suggested in this book that such practices do not necessarily have the desired effect. Once a summative mark is involved for an assessment, that assessment becomes summative assessment irrespective of the intended formative nature of the activity – the student perception and attitude will change. Encouraging student participation and advocating the value of the formative activity may be what people are trying to achieve by giving the summative carrot, but the fact remains that when we give marks which subsequently count towards an academic judgement, or progression decision, then the assessment is summative.

WHY STUDENTS WANT FEEDBACK

Teachers in higher education put a great deal of time and effort into producing written, and indeed, oral feedback. We have already seen that there is a huge amount of assessment and a growing number of students. Despite the changing environment of mass education students want the feedback process to be clear, explicit and fair (Holmes and Smith, 2003). If feedback is to contribute to student learning and we put a great deal of effort into it – how can we be sure that it is having the desired effect on helping students?

A number of commentators on learning and assessment suggest that feedback has the potential to have a significant impact on student learning (for example, Hattie, 1987; Sadler, 1998; Stefani, 1998; Yorke, 2003). Perhaps the simplest reason that students want feedback is that it will help them to learn. However, it is not quite as simple as that. The situation is also further complicated in that the types of feedback which are most effective will vary between disciplines. We need to make sure that the feedback that we provide will actually be useful and usable for students; by this we mean that feedback should:

Be understandable by students

There are a number of levels where there is possibility for misunderstanding of feedback:

- It could be that the students haven't understood what teachers expected from them in the assignment.

43

- It could be that students have different perceptions from teachers of what is expected in the assignment.
- Students might not understand the feedback comments because they either are not detailed enough or are unclear (tendencies to drop into shorthand or education-speak – teachers might understand this but students are likely not to).

Lea and Street (1998) suggest that a great deal of the feedback provided for students is often not understood by the students. Glover and Brown (2006: 12) summarise the understandability issues in that 'such failure [failure to understand feedback comments and/or assessment criteria] inhibits the possibility of any feedback being used in a formative manner'. Nicol and Macfarlane-Dick (2004) suggest that 'one way of increasing the effectiveness of external feedback and the likelihood that the information provided is understood is to conceptualise feedback more as a dialogue rather than as information transmission'. The concept of feedback dialogue will be returned to later in this chapter.

Be valued by students

In order to be valued by students feedback should be constructive and reflect the effort that they have put into any assessment activities but also be meaningful in the context of their future learning needs (feed-forward).

'Close the gap' on their understanding

Hall and Burke (2003: 10) suggest that if students 'know what to do to improve they can "close the gap" between what they can do or know and what they need to do or know'. Hall and Burke go on to argue that 'it is better to focus on causes of success and failure than to praise performance on the basis of the final product or completed task'. Providing feedback which allows students to 'close the gap' is part of what Yorke (2003) alludes to in his discussion of feedback changing student behaviour. Feedback that you provide for your students should address complex learning issues, such as quality of argument, completeness of discussion or interpretation of literature, rather than focus on simple feedback such as exceeding word count or spelling and grammar.

Be of appropriate quality

Black and Wiliam (1998) provide evidence that suggests that the 'quality of feedback given to learners has a significant impact on the quality of learning'. Nicol and Macfarlane-Dick (2004: 11) define good quality feedback as 'information that helps students trouble-shoot their own performance and take action to close the gap between intent and effect'. Quality feedback should be relevant to the formative assessment and to the student learning process.

Be timely

If students don't get the feedback soon enough then feedback is less likely to be perceived to be useful for their ongoing studies. Cowan (2003) suggests that research indicates that feedback needs to be provided 'within minutes' of completing a task in order to be the most effective. Brown *et al.* (1997) also highlight that feedback is at its most effective when it is 'timely, relevant and meaningful'.

Provide an opportunity for dialogue

As we shall see later in this chapter it is suggested that feedback should be able to be used as a catalyst for dialogue between teacher and students and between students.

As well as needing to ensure the 'appropriateness' (encapsulating all of the above) of feedback there is the issue of what students do with the feedback. The literature on the subject does not always paint a particularly rosy picture. Some of the literature on feedback suggests that many students don't really want feedback at all. Some (Hounsell, 1987; Ecclestone, 1998) suggest students usually don't read feedback. Others (Ding, 1998; Adams *et al.*, 2000) conclude that many students only want a grade or mark. Unfortunately, this may indicate that feedback is seen as a quantitative recognition of achievement rather than a qualitative discourse to be acted upon.

A comprehensive study conducted by MacLellan (2001) revealed that students generally view the feedback process as 'only sometimes helpful', with 30 per cent in MacLellan's study indicating that feedback '*never* helps them to understand'. MacLellan goes on to suggest that her findings indicate that there is a discrepancy between students and lecturers as to what constitutes helpful feedback. Much of this discrepancy in perception centres around the way feedback promotes discourse and discussion – 63 per cent of lecturers thought that feedback prompts discussion between student and teacher whereas only 2 per cent of students responded positively to the same question. Indeed 50 per cent of students suggested that feedback never prompted discussion.

Nicol and Macfarlane-Dick (2004: 4) argue that 'any model of feedback must take account of the way students make sense of, and use, feedback information'. In order to for us to understand how students actually make sense of the feedback we provide them and appreciate how they use it, we need to examine in a little more detail why students want feedback at all. We shall discuss the learning and teaching rationale for providing feedback in a moment, but there are other pragmatic issues we need to take into account, such as:

■ Students feel that it is only fair that they are provided with feedback after they have put in the effort to complete the assessment; students expect feedback as they 'believe they deserve it' due to the effort made in carrying out the assignment task (Higgins *et al.*, 2001).

■ Higgins *et al.* (2001) also suggest that students view feedback as part of the service they have paid for!

■ Gibbs (2005) raises the concern that this consumer awareness may manifest itself in an increasing amount of student complaint, appeal and even litigation.

One positive aspect to come out of this type of issue is raised by Higgins *et al.* (2001) who suggest that the emerging consumerist awareness of students leads them to understand the importance of feedback in their educational development. So perhaps we can even use this to our advantage, letting students know that they are paying for the feedback – so they should use it!

A significant part of the problem with encouraging students to engage with feedback appears to occur when marks are provided at the same time as feedback comments. Students tend to perceive marks as an indication of their academic ability and poor marks can have a demoralising and demotivating impact on their self-belief.

Feedback also tends to be perceived as an indication of how students tackled a particular task and is not perceived as in indicator on how to improve or how to feedforward. We shall return to this issue in Chapter 3 when we discuss reflective learning.

Time Out

► Is student demand for feedback – 'as part of the service' – becoming a common experience?

► How many times have your students complained because they put so much time and effort into a piece of work only to receive a small amount of written feedback?

Students need to know what to do with feedback comments in order to use the feedback to enhance their learning. Sadler (1989) indicates that in order for students to appreciate feedback and construct actions to deal with the feedback they need to 'possess some of the same evaluative skills as their teacher'. Others suggest the need for students to have self-assessment skills (Boud, 2000; Yorke, 2003). Developing skills in self-assessment (Sambell, 1999; McDonald and Boud, 2003) will help in the deconstruction of formative feedback and will help students learn from the feedback process. Developing skills in self-assessment will also help the student develop the skills required for independent learning.

Despite the negative arguments against feedback there are many positive arguments expounding the benefits of feedback. As we've seen in Chapter 1 Stefani (1998) argues that supportive feedback, both oral and written, when it is given in a supportive and constructive way is a vital element for student learning and Hattie (1987) indicates that the most powerful influence on student achievement is feedback.

Earlier in this chapter, the motivational aspects of feedback were discussed and it was shown that feedback can act as a source of motivation for students both by lifting student morale through the provision of feedback (dispositional) or using feedback to focus on emphasising when students do well and correct performance is reinforced (epistomological).

There are many reasons for students wanting feedback – many realise that if there is constructive and developmental feedback, it will help their understanding and enhance their learning. The following list provides some of the positive uses of feedback from a student perspective:

- Students make use of feedback to learn.
- Students use the feedback to 'close the gap' on their learning requirements and their subject understanding.

47

- Students use formative feedback to help them prepare for summative assessments (this formative feedback can be from the previous summative assessment – and brings into play the need for timely feedback, see Chapter 3 for more discussion on this issue).
- Students can be motivated by feedback.
- Students use feedback to appreciate the expected academic standards – for example in addressing level of academic requirement or understanding specific issues such as plagiarism. It is much better to address issues such as plagiarism in a formative environment than in a summative situation where the consequences for the student may be substantial. Unfortunately, in obtaining feedback (this is better to happen in a formative situation than a summative one), it is often the first time students become aware of the seriousness of plagiarism and other academic misconducts.
- Students are encouraged to try things out.
- Students can use feedback as input to reflective learning and as examples or input for their Personal Development Plans – addressed in Chapter 3.

 Time Out

▶ What do your students tell you is good about the feedback you give them?

▶ You might like to consider this from a number of perspectives:

   i)   what they say to you
   ii) what they say to their peers, or possibly
   iii) what they say to Staff Student Liaison Committees or Quality Assurance Review.

▶ What opportunities do your students have to discuss feedback with you?

COMMUNICATING WITH YOUR STUDENTS ABOUT FEEDBACK – ENTERING INTO DIALOGUE

It is important that when we give feedback to students we are very clear with students that it is not our role to spoon-feed them and to 'make them do things' but to make their learning possible (Ramsden, 1992). In order for students to benefit from formative assessment and formative feedback students must have the opportunity to express and communicate their understanding of the feedback that they receive. Higgins *et al.* (2001) argue that we need to 'pay more attention to feedback as a process of communication'. Nicol and Macfarlane-Dick (2004: 7) suggest that 'feedback as dialogue means that the student not only receives initial feedback but also has the opportunity to engage the teacher in discussion about that feedback'.

Before even giving any feedback it is important that we discuss the concept of feedback with the students to help them understand:

- What constitutes feedback – ironically students often fail to recognise that verbal discussion on their work is feedback.
- What type of feedback they can expect.
- When they can expect their feedback.

Rust (2002) indicates that a review of research literature suggests that 'just giving feedback to students without requiring them to actively engage with it is likely to have only limited effect [on student learning and understanding]'. As well as thinking about what it is we are providing in feedback we should be thinking about ways to encourage students to engage with this feedback.

We should endeavour to encourage students to:

- think about the activities on which they have received feedback;
- engage in dialogue with tutors;
- think about the type of feedback they want and they need in order to enhance their learning; and
- take ownership of their learning.

If we are to find out whether students are learning from the feedback we provide, we need to either engage in dialogue with them about the feedback or use the feedback as input to a future task (feedforward or as input to reflective learning).

We can also take the opportunity to obtain feedback on the quality of the feedback we provide. For example, by discussing with students how the feedback we have provided helps in their learning. (At the Open University, examination of the feedback is done independently from the teacher who provides the feedback.) It might seem a little strange trying to obtain feedback on feedback, but getting student feedback on the formative

49

assessment activities, and the formative feedback provided on these activities, can contribute a very positive input to our understanding of the effectiveness of our feedback and indeed what it is (assuming that it is something) that students have learned from the activity (we shall return to this in Chapter 6).

The way we communicate with students about their feedback can have motivating and potentially demotivating consequences. If feedback is given constructively and openly it can give students the confidence to ask questions, to discuss their work and find out more about their subject as well as any errors or misconceptions they might have. However, if we fail to enter into open dialogue, we can put students off – even if it's only the impression students take away, if they feel we haven't time for them or can't be bothered it can have a serious, long-lasting negative impact.

There are a number of techniques which can be used to encourage dialogue based on feedback, such as:

- Getting students to indicate in advance the type of feedback they would like and in which particular areas they would like feedback.
- Getting students to identify in advance of the feedback what they think went well, what went badly and what they learned from participating in the exercise (see case study on student engagement).
- Getting students to identify feedback that they found helpful – asking them why it was helpful (this will help you in reflecting on your feedback practice) – possibly encouraging them to write about what they learned from feedback in their follow-on activities (encourages feedforward).
- Giving feedback at a different time from giving the mark (for example, give the mark 2 weeks after you have given the feedback).
- Encouraging students to develop action plans as a result of feedback – helps with engagement and in considering how to 'close the gap'.
- Utilising peer-assessment and peer feedback (see Chapter 4).

SUMMARY

If students are to engage in formative assessment and formative feedback (attending to the feedback when it is received and acting upon that feedback) there is a need to ensure that the formative activities are valued by the students. In order for the activities to be valued the contribution to the students' learning and the reward for the effort put in by the students needs to be clear and explicit (attempts to move away from marks as reward are encouraged, with reward being a self-perception by students that they have learned).

In order to allow space and time for formative activities there needs to be a reduction in the amount of summative assessment, which requires a culture shift in institutions by programme teams, by teachers and by students.

In order to understand how to encourage students to engage in formative activities we need to understand a little bit about what motivates and drives them in their learning and what it is that they perceive as valuable in their education.

As teachers we need to appreciate that we are teaching very diverse groups of students with different learning needs, different approaches to learning and different motivations for engaging in learning.

Chapter 3

Using formative assessment and formative feedback in learning and teaching

CHAPTER SUMMARY

This chapter will examine and discuss methods and techniques for using formative assessment and formative feedback in learning and teaching in terms of what it might mean for your teaching practice – and of course how your teaching practice will enhance student learning and student learning opportunities. Particular emphasis will be placed on the design of formative activities which encourage dialogue between students and between students and teachers as well as how to use formative activities to provide feedforward learning opportunities. The design of effective and efficient formative activities will be discussed with reference to learning outcomes, pragmatics and workload – taking into account student understanding of feedback and whether the key to feedback is quality or quantity.

INTRODUCTION

Formative assessment is not just about assessment, and formative feedback is not just about giving feedback – which is why in this book the term 'formative activity' is used. Formative assessment and formative feedback are also about teaching practice – the focus of this chapter – and about providing opportunities for student learning in our teaching activities. The purpose of this chapter is to apply the principles and theories considered in Chapters 1 and 2 to your teaching practice.

One of the key issues in the design of formative activities is to encourage dialogue between teachers and students, and between students.

It is suggested in this chapter that giving consideration to the design of formative activities and how you will integrate formative assessment and formative feedback into your teaching practice will enhance your teaching practice and provide opportunities for you to consider how to make your teaching more effective. This enhancement will take place as a result of the fact that you are actively reflecting on and considering your teaching practice, irrespective of whether you implement formative activities or not.

In the design of formative activities you need to consider what it is you are trying to achieve in terms both of how the activities will improve student learning and of how they will improve the student experience.

 Teaching Tip

It is suggested in this book that in order to use formative activities to enhance your teaching and provide effective learning opportunities for students the formative activities need to be carefully planned and fully integrated into your modules and programmes. It is important that students are informed about the types of formative activities, the timing of the formative activities and how they will benefit from participating in and engaging with those formative activities. To that end it is suggested that you define your formative activities in your teaching plans or schedules and communicate these to students, for example in module guides and introduction to modules.

We need to consider a number of issues about how we integrate formative activities into our learning and teaching, particularly in terms of:

- quality and quantity of feedback
- timeliness/immediacy of feedback
- value (perceived and actual) of formative activities, and
- workload for both teachers and students.

WHY DO WE 'DO' FEEDBACK – WHO IS IT FOR?

In order to integrate formative activities into your teaching you need to be clear in your own mind (and also clarify with your students – preferably through dialogue) why you are providing feedback, what the intended purpose of the feedback is and how the feedback relates to other teaching interventions.

There is a danger that you will be producing feedback because you think you should be doing it as part of your job, and you end up actually producing the feedback to satisfy yourself (this may sound a little bit off the wall, especially when you consider the amount of time you spend in generating feedback). Part of this situation may arise because your institution expects you to produce feedback as part of a learning and teaching strategy, as part of your workload or to be used as evidence for external examiners or external review.

While these reasons no doubt have some value and some element of rationale we need to focus on providing feedback for students and consider the ways in which students will benefit from our feedback and how our feedback will add value to the student learning experience.

When we consider that we are producing feedback for students it will help us think about the type of feedback we provide and the language we use in that feedback (see Chapter 4 for examples of good and not-so-good practice). If we provide feedback for external examiners – to show that we've considered student work then writing 'evidence' on a script might indicate that we consider there to be an issue with evidence and that might be enough of an intervention (alternatively it might just be there to show the external examiner that we have read the script and we are making some sort of comment). However, imagine yourself as a student reading the comment 'evidence'. It could be interpreted in a number of different ways, including:

- This is an example of evidence.
- Do you intend this to be evidence?
- This evidence is good.
- This evidence is not detailed enough.
- More evidence is expected to justify your assertion.

There are probably many more interpretations!

 Time Out

► Who do you really produce your feedback for?

► If it is for students, what steps do you take to ensure that students understand the point you are making?

► How will your feedback help students to learn?

An example that attempts to illustrate the potential dilemma of whom we provide feedback for is given below.

Consider the feedback from students about the feedback you provide and consider feedback from external examiners about the same feedback.

External examiners may consider the feedback to be excellent:

a)   because it is there;
b)   because it indicates that the work has been marked fairly and consistently (indicator of assessment reliability); and
c)   because it maps the students' success against a series of learning outcomes.

On the other hand, student feedback on the same feedback could conceivably be:

a)   don't know/didn't get any feedback — they said my work was given to the external examiner;
b)   didn't understand any of the comments about learning outcomes;
c)   feedback was fine, but I needed it much earlier, before I sat my end-of-module examination.

QUALITY OR QUANTITY

We discussed students' expectations in Chapter 2 and as we indicated, students expect a certain amount of feedback. How many times have students complained because they put so much time and effort into a piece of work only to receive a small amount of written feedback? (As an aside, it is a little disconcerting to realise that many students don't regard verbal comments on activities, either formative or summative, as actual feedback!)

Quality feedback should be relevant to the formative assessment and to the student learning process. Quality of feedback can be measured in a number of ways, such as timeliness, relevance, level of information, degree to which feedback encourages student learning and quantity (too little or too much). Nicol and Macfarlane-Dick (2004: 11) define good quality feedback as 'information that helps students trouble-shoot their own performance and take action to close the gap between intent and effect'.

Nicol and Macfarlane-Dick (2004: 11) go on to suggest that a great deal of 'feedback information is often about strengths and weaknesses of handed-in work or about aspects of performance that are easy to identify (such as spelling mistakes) rather than about aspects that are of greater importance to academic learning but that are more abstract and difficult to define (such as strength of argument)'.

As far as quantity is concerned, Lunsford (1997) advocates that there should be a maximum of three well-thought-out comments per essay or report. Lunsford also argues that feedback should relate to students how the reader 'experienced the essay . . . rather than offer judgemental comments'. The intention is that such comments help the student to engage in reflecting on the feedback and trying to understand, as Lunsford puts it, 'the difference between his or her intentions and the effects'.

USING FORMATIVE ACTIVITIES IN YOUR TEACHING

Using formative activities in your teaching has a number of objectives – all of which aim to enhance the student learning experience without the pressure of summative assessment. We have already discussed that students may be resistant to formative activities because of other demands and pressures on their time, but this is one of the challenges facing teachers in HE – to encourage participation in formative activities and to reduce the amount of time spent on summative activities. Irons and Alexander (2004: 9) take this further, arguing that one of the challenges in learning and teaching in HE is to incorporate assessment techniques that 'can be used to improve formative feedback while at the same time encourage students to take responsibility for their academic learning'.

The use of formative activities in your teaching will hopefully encourage students to take an active involvement in their learning and indeed take responsibility for that learning – encouraging students to take active involvement in their learning is advocated by the Assessment Reform Group (1999).

Implicit in getting students to take responsibility for their learning is the need to develop skill in self-assessment. Formative activities will provide opportunities to practice self-assessment. Embedding self-assessment will help students make more effective use of formative feedback – particularly in appreciating what students need to do to 'close the gap' in their understanding. Self-assessment will also prove beneficial in providing a starting point for dialogue between students, and between students and their teachers. The ability to self-assess will also help students when it comes to participating in peer-assessment – both in providing constructive assessment for their peers and in receiving feedback from their peers.

When formative activities are used constructively in your teaching – both formative assessment and formative feedback – there can be a positive impact on raising students' self esteem and belief in their abilities to cope in higher education. This is particularly important in an increasingly diverse student population.

The structure of programmes and modules often means that there is little time for teachers to utilise formative activities either because of very full curricula or because of the size of modules and the short time span associated with these modules. Gibbs (2005) suggests that many institutions are moving towards larger modules and year-long modules (as opposed to semester based) but that there are also difficulties in changing to structures which will help with formative activities because of university regulations. The author would also add that administrative inertia and resistance to change also provide challenges in moving to structures which allow for formative development.

We also come up against issues in lack of participation because of student perceptions regarding the value of formative activities. As discussed in Chapter 2 it would appear that students are motivated by summative assessment and are less likely to engage in formative activities if they perceive that they are not getting any reward for participating in those activities.

TIMELINESS OF FEEDBACK

Cowan (2003) suggests that research indicates that feedback needs to be provided 'within minutes' of completing a task in order to be the most effective. Brown *et al.* (1997) also highlight that feedback is at its most effective when it is 'timely, relevant and meaningful'. Regular feedback can be seen to have a positive impact on students' academic performance. Research undertaken by Tuckman (1999) suggests a link between providing students with regular feedback on academic performance and an improvement in subsequent academic performance.

The natural reaction from you as a teacher would quite rightly be that the desire for immediacy of feedback is almost impossible to fulfil, especially in the context of increasing student numbers and heavy workload. However, careful design of formative activities, sampling strategies (see Chapter 4), utilisation of ICTs (see Chapter 5) to help us, or getting students to be involved through peer- or self-assessment can help us manage workload issues and at the same time provide students with constructive and timely feedback.

DESIGN OF FORMATIVE ACTIVITIES

In Chapter 2 we discussed the issues associated with student engagement in formative activities. An important consideration in ensuring that students perceive the activities to be valuable is to take great care in the design of the activities. Key to adding value is to design the activities in such a way that students understand how they contribute to student learning and that they are integral part of learning in teaching, irrespective of the level that the activities are aligned to, be it teaching session, module, level or whole programme.

A useful starting point for the design of formative activities is to consider how they will:

a) empower students to learn;
b) motivate students to engage and participate; and
c) be valued by students as part of their learning and education.

This of course needs to be balanced against staff workload and other pragmatic considerations, such as timeliness.

There are many types of formative assessment that can be utilised in the design of formative activities. The underlying principles in selecting the most appropriate types should be:

- to align the activity with the desired learning outcome;
- to encourage dialogue between tutors and students; and
- to provide opportunities for timely and constructive feedback.

Typical formative assessment activities include:

- practical exercises
- tutorials
- drafts of assessments
- project supervisions
- group discussions and groupwork
- student demonstrations
- student presentations
- portfolios
- reflective log books, and
- diagnostic interviews and tests.

There is also a range of formative feedback mechanisms that should be considered in the design of the formative activity. Again, the most appropriate to use will depend on the circumstances, but the following list illustrates typical feedback approaches (other more detailed examples of good feedback practice are provided in Chapter 4):

- annotated scripts (coursework and examinations)
- feedback sheets
- marking grids
- model answers
- statement banks
- demonstrations
- peer feedback
- tutorials, and
- various e-assessment mechanisms (see Chapter 5).

The type of formative feedback used will depend on the teaching environment and the circumstances associated with the student group and the specific subject matter being addressed in the formative assessment.

Research undertaken at the author's institution identified the following factors which will have an impact on the most appropriate type of formative feedback to use:

- the size of student cohort;
- the influence of external bodies (such as external examiners, Professional and Statutory Regulatory Bodies (PSRBs), employers);
- the ability to evaluate the effectiveness of the formative feedback on student learning;
- the extent to which formative activities are linked to PDPs.

Knight (2001: 6) suggests that 'good formative assessment means designing learning sequences that afford plenty of opportunities for good learning conversations arising from feedback on good tasks that are matched to course learning outcomes'. In effect this means that in designing your formative activities you should consider how the assessment and the feedback will facilitate feedforward to allow for students to use the formative activities in their future activities. While feedback aims to close the gap on understanding, if it is only used by students as a set of comments on student work, then there may well be problems (as discussed in

Chapters 1 and 2) of getting students to engage with the feedback (even to get students to read the feedback, never mind act on it) and act on the feedback. If feedback is actually feedforward – i.e. helps close a gap in future understanding or learning needs, then the enhancement to overall student learning will be more pronounced and more effective.

This also means that the feedback has to be understandable to students and have constructive meaning. Lea and Street (1998) suggest that students often have difficulty in understanding feedback (either in terms of language used or in relation to the tasks the students have undertaken) and are not always able to use the feedback to enhance their learning. Havranek (2002) explores the importance of using appropriate language in feedback in order to facilitate student understanding.

 Teaching Tip

Formative assessment activities and formative feedback should be integrated fully into your teaching and one way to achieve this is to ensure that your formative activities are aligned to module learning outcomes and where possible indicate where and how they contribute to programme learning outcomes.

In a modularised programme there is a danger that student perception of learning focuses on modules and students do not necessarily appreciate the concepts of prerequisite or post-acquisite learning outcomes in modules. It is often the case that students, and for that matter academic staff, see modules as autonomous, standalone blocks. In order for feedback and feedforward to be most effective a holistic view of the curriculum, where modules feed into each other, is required.

A holistic approach is often difficult to achieve under a modular system – but when it is embraced, then feedback at the end of a module may increase in value when it feeds forward into another module.

Formative feedback and formative assessment activities should be designed to help students learn from their activities and in particular identify what needs to be done to improve their knowledge and under-standing. This can be done either as a learning activity in its own right or as preparation for summative assessment. Using formative assessment as preparation for summative assessment (for example, using mock exam questions) might seem to go against the arguments put forward in this book about reducing the amount of summative assessment and about the over reliance on summative assessment. However, we do need to be pragmatic and realise that summative assessment is going to exist in one form or another for some time to come. Using formative assessment and feedback to help students prepare for their summative assessment, through outline structures, draft work, mock questions or other methods, will at least provide the opportunity for guidance and potentially discussion about assessment and help student performance in the summative assessment.

Formative feedback can also be provided on summative assessments and this type of feedback can help the process of learning from the assessment. This is often the main source of 'formal' formative feedback in the eyes of the students.

In the scenario where there is a series (this series could be two pieces of assessment) of summative assessments contributing to a particular learning outcome (either in a module or at a programme level) it is important that formative feedback on the summative work helps the student learn for the next summative assessment – the principle of feedforward. The feedback need not be confined to learning outcomes but could also be more generic in nature, contributing to other learning outcomes or to generic academic expectations or to transferable skills. Getting feedback to students before the next related task has implications for the quality and timeliness of the feedback as well as the timing of summative assessment hand-in dates.

Feedback on end-of-module assessments can be particularly problematic – especially when students do not make the connection between modules and do not see how feedback from one module might help on another. There is also a problem with the situation when students are referred in a module. Normally students will be referred over the summer period with results and instructions regarding the referral being sent to them at the beginning of that period. It is important also that students get feedback on why they did not pass and what they can do before attempting or submitting the referral. We need to think about why students have not done so well and what we can do to help them – especially when we are having that well-earned holiday or doing research away from the office.

 Time Out

▶ How do you support students who have been referred in your modules?

▶ How can we help referred students close the gap?

In designing your formative assessment and formative assessment activities there are a number of pragmatic issues to take into account. As indicated in the introduction to this chapter these include:

- quality and quantity of feedback (including understandability and usability of the feedback);
- timeliness/immediacy of feedback;
- value (perceived and actual) of formative activities; and
- workload for both teachers and students.

In designing formative assessments (and for that matter in designing summative assessments) we should consider a number of factors. It should go without saying that the educational objective of the activity should be clearly thought out and the activity designed in such a way as to achieve the desired outcomes of the activity (from both teacher and student perspective). However, in the context of this book we should consider how we design the activities in such a way as to give us the opportunity to provide speedy, constructive and helpful feedback.

We should make every attempt to address the following:

- Ensure that the formative activities have clear objectives – when we consider the design of formative activities we need to think about student participation and what value the students will place on the activity. One way to do this is to be clear about the objectives of the activity. (Clarifying objectives will also help in enhancing the design of summative assessment activities.)
- Design activities which allow for subject based feedback (and potentially feedback on transferable skills, see later in the chapter) which is constructive and can be given quickly and easily.
- Consider ways in which the formative activity will encourage students to discuss their work either with you or with other students. You can design activities in such a way that the dialogue happens after students have done the work but you can also engage students beforehand, either in negotiating criteria or in getting students to tell you what areas they would like you to give them feedback on.
- Provide feedback which students can use to identify strengths and areas for development (allow students to close the gap on their understanding).

- Provide comments and guidance which students can utilise for feedforward. A great deal depends on the nature of the curriculum and syllabus and the scheduling of the formative activities. This is often an issue in modularised programmes. However, one way to address the issue is to encourage students to develop action plans.
- Link the formative assessment and formative feedback to other PDP activities – particularly when reflective components are embedded. Linking to PDP also allows students to consider the development of their transferable and key skills.
- Provide opportunities for peer-assessment and feedback and also self-assessment where appropriate.
- In designing your formative activities you may choose to be innovative and give students the freedom to discuss with you before you provide feedback and determine the areas they would like to have feedback provided on.

These suggestions do not need to be applied in isolation – indeed it would be most appropriate to combine the suggestions in any given formative activity.

ENCOURAGING DIALOGUE AND CONVERSATIONS

In Chapter 2 we discussed the benefits associated with entering into discourse with students about their feedback. The principle sounds reasonable – but what about the pragmatics and the practical aspects?

In designing formative activities we can build in opportunities for students to explain their thinking or their work. This can include formative assessment activities such as the reading aloud of an essay, giving a presentation, explaining a design or artefact or outlining a prototype. The viva voce has long been a summative assessment instrument for final year undergraduate projects, Masters dissertations and doctoral examinations. We can adapt the principles of the viva voce and use these as a means for discussion, discourse and dialogue in formative activities.

It is important, if discussion and dialogue around formative activities are to be successful and constructive, that we promote discussion, help students accept discussion as the norm and develop a learning culture of open discussion (acceptance of critical comment from teachers and peers). We can make use of activities (and time) in practicals/seminars and tutorials to discuss and deconstruct feedback.

63

When we are engaging in dialogue with students or encouraging students to work together in providing peer feedback it is important that we allow students appropriate time to discuss feedback. At the same time it is important that we take away any perceived stigma of getting things wrong. One of the great benefits of formative assessment is that the pressure of 'getting things right' is taken away and students have more opportunity to learn by trying things out and learning from making errors and mistakes.

Encouraging dialogue will also give students (and you) the confidence to identify and discuss examples of feedback that helped them. This will also potentially be useful feedback for you about your teaching practice (see Chapter 6 for more discussion).

DEVELOPING EFFECTIVE FEEDBACK

In order for feedback to be effective it needs to be provided quickly – Race (1995) suggests feedback is best when it is instantaneous. The ability to provide timely feedback will be shaped by the way we design formative activities.

In considering how to provide effective feedback it is important to remember how the formative activities that we are giving feedback on are aligned to learning outcomes. This will help address the issue of students understanding the feedback in relation to the tasks they have been set. This of course assumes that the learning outcomes are clear and are communicated to the students.

The learning outcomes can be used as criteria for giving feedback but other predefined criteria can also be utilised. So in providing effective feedback the feedback is mapped against that predefined criteria. One approach that can be effective in using predefined criteria is to make use of tick box sheets (see the example below). These sheets are particularly effective when combined with dialogue and discourse – for example in giving feedback on a student presentation or demonstration.

Learning Outcome 1				
Beyond expectation	Fully met	Met	Partially met	Not met
Comment				

In order to provide effective feedback we need to consider the clarity of feedback, especially how we indicate the ways in which students can improve and develop for the future (feedforward). This is not simply a case of pointing out errors or faults and expecting students to sort out what is required, but an indication of the steps students can take in order to 'close the gap' on their understanding or by focusing on key areas for development and improvement.

INCLUSIVENESS AND DIVERSITY

We indicated earlier in this chapter that feedback should be provided for students and focus on the students' learning needs. In mass education systems, such as today's higher education provision, we need to remember that not all students are the same, the learning needs for students will vary and there will be a wide range of student learning experiences.

As with all educational activities there is a need to consider the nature of formative assessment and formative feedback for diverse student groups, taking into account legislation such as the Disability Discrimination Act (DDA) (1995) and the Special Education Needs and Discrimination Act (SENDA) (2001).

The needs of other groups of students, such as international and mature students, also need to be taken into account in the design of formative assessment and the provision of formative feedback.

Formative assessment and formative feedback provide us with an opportunity to address inclusiveness and diversity. There has been a large amount of work on diversity undertaken by the Higher Education Academy work (for example, HEFCE, 2002; Higher Education Academy, 2006) and from organisations such as the National Disability Team (see www.techdis. ac.uk). However, the vast majority of this work focuses on teaching practice or on summative assessment rather than on formative assessment or formative feedback.

A great deal of the work on diversity has been reactive in nature – i.e. we are aware of a student or group of students with particular needs and we put in place mechanisms to allow the students to participate equally in the assessment (be it summative or formative). However, if we are more proactive and consider inclusiveness for all students when we are designing our activities then the reliance on a reactive approach should diminish. The process of addressing diversity in assessment and attempting to make assessment inclusive can be of benefit to all students as we consider in detail the expectations we place on the assessment, the impact of the assessment on the students and the potential problems that may arise from the assessment.

It is suggested that equality and diversity issues can be proactively addressed by addressing the inclusiveness of assessment activities – both summative and formative. Addressing inclusiveness will be a benefit for all students because, if the improved levels of consideration are given to the assessment design and the mechanisms for feedback as well as to improving the clarity in specifying assessment tasks, the activity will be enhanced for all.

 Time Out

▶ Who uses it most/who needs it most?

▶ How do you investigate who most needs feedback?

▶ Can you develop strategies which give feedback to those who need it most?

ENCOURAGING REFLECTIVE PRACTICE

Reflective learning is a key skill associated with independent learning and is also a key skill for employability. The key components of reflective learning are outlined in Kolb's (1984) experiential learning cycle. Formative assessment can be used to establish Kolb's 'concrete experience' allowing students to participate at a personal level in a particular task. Formative feedback can be used to inform the 'reflective observation' as part of the systematic reflection on that experience or learning opportunity. This is especially powerful when tutor or peer feedback is compared with student self-assessment. Formative feedback can also be used to provide guidance on the 'abstract conceptualisation'. This is often the part of Kolb's cycle that students find most difficult and therefore it is important to provide constructive and helpful feedback to enable students to use the feedback alongside theories and principles (subject specific or generic) to develop an appropriate level of understanding. The final part of Kolb's cycle, 'active experimentation', encourages students to try things out based on formative assessment experience, the resultant feedback and the analysis of that feedback. It is suggested that at this stage students are encouraged to examine what went well, what went badly, what they'd do differently if they had to participate in a similar concrete experience.

Irons and Smailes (2006) have adapted Kolb's learning cycle to illustrate the ways in which formative assessment and formative feedback can be utilised in order to encourage reflection and provide learning opportunities from the formative assessment activities.

TRANSFERABLE SKILLS, PERSONAL DEVELOPMENT PLANS (PDPS) AND FORMATIVE ASSESSMENT AND FEEDBACK

In the discussion thus far we have focused on formative activities and formative feedback specifically at a subject based level. Indeed it has been intimated (and is again discussed in Chapter 4) that providing feedback on issues such as spelling, grammar, presentation style etc. is a bit of a 'cop out' in terms of using formative activities to enhance student learning. That said, there is an expectation that transferable skills are also developed as part of the student learning experience and as such we should provide feedback and guidance on transferable skills as well as subject based activities. The incorporation and development of key or transferable skills is an important and integral part of education in HE, as emphasised in the Dearing Report (1997) (see NCIHE, 1997).

There was a government expectation for PDPs to be integrated into the curriculum in universities by 2005. PDPs offer an opportunity to address many of the issues associated with a restrictive culture of summative assessment and move to a more open, invigorating and motivating culture where formative and developmental feedback is provided to students, where students are responsible for their own learning and students use PDPs as evidence of that learning.

We need to consider how to develop formative activities which will develop transferable skills and how to incorporate feedback which will help in transferable skills development and decide whether these should stand alone in terms of developing transferable skills or be contextualised within the subject domain. Whether you design activities to focus on transferable skills or to embed them is really up to you. The important thing is to make clear to students what the activity is designed to do. A mixed approach is often the most appropriate, for instance see the example below.

Students from different backgrounds clearly have different study patterns and skills. Programmes of study in HE need to develop the skills required for graduates in employment, i.e. transferable skills as well as subject specific skills and knowledge. Transferable skills are an important component of the employability skills set. It is not always the case that key skills are explicitly stated, taught or assessed in their own right.

67

EXAMPLE

This exercise will give you the opportunity to develop your appreciation of:

The factors impacting on systems security – aligned to learning outcome 1 in your module descriptor and your presentation skills when you deliver a 5-minute summary of your findings.

You will have the opportunity to discuss feedback on both the issues around systems security and your presentation skills.

There are many issues involved in the teaching of transferable skills and these issues are often exacerbated as a result of modular academic structures. Transferable skills need to be applied across the whole curriculum, and with modularisation there is a real danger that such skills are restricted to a few core modules or omitted completely. Students must be presented with the opportunity to practise and develop their transferable skills, i.e. problem solving, communication, literacy, group work, producing executive summaries, critical analysis and giving presentations. Students need formative feedback in order to develop these skills.

The introduction of PDPs may well provide the impetus to encourage reflection on skills development and encourage students to participate in formative activities which will help in the development of their transferable skills. Using PDPs as a mechanism for learning allows students to demonstrate deep learning through practice and reflection. As with formative assessment and formative feedback it is important that PDP development should not be seen as an extra task but be integrated into the curriculum.

It is possible to link PDPs (including formative feedback which is collated and reflected upon in the PDP) to policies on guidance tutoring, which in turn have a positive impact on retention. Using PDPs as a focus for the guidance tutorial has a number of positive effects, both for the development of the PDP and for the value of the guidance tutorial – it encourages students to participate in formative activities and engage in creating their PDPs, adds value to the PDP and provides common context and evidence for the guidance tutorial.

SUMMARY – WHAT DOES IT MEAN FOR YOUR TEACHING PRACTICE?

In this chapter we have discussed a number of methods and techniques for how you might incorporate formative assessment and formative feedback into your teaching practice. The following guidelines summarise the main points discussed in the chapter and form a framework for you to consider when designing and implementing your formative activities:

1) Consider when formative assessment and formative feedback will be used in teaching and learning.

2) Be clear what the objectives of the formative activities are.

3) Specify in module descriptor of when and in what format formative assessment and formative feedback will take place.

4) Include formative assessment and formative feedback in teaching scheme/schedule provided to students so that students are aware of timings.

5) Explain the purpose of the formative activities to students.

6) Discuss how the formative activities are designed to contribute to the student learning experience in the module.

7) Consider how formative activities will:
    a) contribute to PDP development;
    b) enhance student learning;
    c) provide useful information for students;
    d) facilitate self- and peer-assessment;
    e) encourage discussion between lecturers and students;
    f) motivate students; and
    g) reduce summative assessment.

8) Design the formative assessment and formative feedback so as to take into account pragmatic issues, such as:
    - the workload involved in designing formative assessment activities;
    - the workload involved in providing the feedback;
    - the level and type of constructive support that can be provided;
    - the opportunity to provide timely feedback; and
    - the opportunity to provide quality feedback that will enhance student learning.

Chapter 4

Formative assessment and feedback techniques

CHAPTER SUMMARY

One of the key issues in advocating formative assessment and formative feedback is the impact that these activities have on academic workload. In this chapter we address ways in which we can provide feedback and manage workload at the same time. A variety of different methods and techniques will be introduced and discussed – looking at good practice and at not-so-good practice. Case studies utilising the tools and techniques across a range of disciplines will be presented in Chapter 7.

INTRODUCTION

The first three chapters in this book have focused on the theoretical underpinnings associated with summative assessment, formative assessment and formative feedback. A number of ideas have been presented and questions asked which hopefully have encouraged you to consider your teaching practice. In this chapter a number of tools and techniques are considered – both good practice and bad practice.

In this chapter we will also consider techniques and tips which will help in managing your workload, and hopefully alleviating some of the strain on your workload – while at the same time enhancing the student learning experience.

In the HE Academy project, Student Enhanced Learning Through Effective Feedback (SENLEF), Juwah *et al.* (2004) promote the following seven principles of good feedback practice:

- facilitates the development of self-assessment (reflection) in learning;
- encourages teacher and peer dialogue around learning;

- helps clarify what good performance is (goals, criteria, expected standards);
- provides opportunities to close the gap between current and desired performance;
- delivers high quality information to students about their learning;
- encourages positive, motivational beliefs and self-esteem;
- provides information to teachers that can be used to help shape teaching.

The examples in this chapter attempt to embrace these principles and provide positive and pragmatic suggestions on how we as teachers and practitioners can improve our formative feedback, taking into account workload constraints and other practical issues.

Details on the SENLEF Project can be found at www.heacademy.ac.uk/senlef.htm.

WAYS TO GIVE FEEDBACK AND MANAGE YOUR WORKLOAD

There are significant workload pressures on academics working in HE. There are a wide variety of expectations that are part of the academic role in HE, including all of which takes up time (this is not an exhaustive list but it illustrates the point):

- research
- income generation
- subject development
- dealing with academic bureaucracy
- embracing e-learning
- promoting innovative pedagogy
- programme management, and
- student pastoral support.

How then can we justify spending time on formative assessment and the production of formative feedback? How can we fit it into an already full workload? The answer is fairly straightforward – we can't! We certainly can't if we are to address all the existing demands and we certainly can't unless we change the time we spend on activities such as the ones indicated above.

71

It might seem that there is a bit of a contradiction here. We are suggesting providing more regular and quicker feedback, advocating discussion with students and providing guidelines on how to improve feedback – surely all this is going to increase workload and the pressure on academics?

In Chapter 1 we suggested a number of strategies which will allow us to free up the time in order to provide formative assessment and formative feedback including:

- reducing the overall amount of summative assessment – which in turn will free up time to spend on constructive formative activities;
- running formative and summative activities in parallel;
- making use of peer- and self-assessment in formative activities, including giving formative feedback.

In the design of formative activities we need to encourage student engagement and enhance student learning without creating the need to do huge amounts of marking or increase already full workloads in other ways. It has been argued earlier in this book that a reduction in summative assessment is to be encouraged and this can be replaced by formative activities. We can attempt to manage workload by adopting approaches which allow us to select or sample student formative work – this can be enhanced by students indicating the work that they would prefer to have feedback on.

Giving feedback takes time, giving constructive and developmental feedback takes more time – there is no way of avoiding this situation. There are, however, a number of techniques which can be utilised in formative assessment activities which will allow us to provide formative feedback without taking inordinate amounts of time. Perhaps the most constructive, and the potentially biggest time saving techniques, are getting students to participate in peer feedback and self-assessment – leading to self-reflection. The following examples illustrate techniques which are manageable in terms of workload and are also beneficial to students.

Perhaps the most obvious approach to avoiding being swamped by the need to provide feedback is to get someone else to provide the feedback for you (or with you). Possible sources of co-option include:

- research assistants or PhD students
- teaching teams

- independent colleagues (expect some payback at a later date!)
- colleagues from industry or business.

Great care needs to be taken in using any of these approaches, to ensure fairness and equality as well as to ensure validity of assessment. It will probably take you a significant amount of effort to put this approach in place and you will benefit from sampling the feedback to ensure consistency.

It is possible to put in place a strategy for students where we don't actually provide feedback on every piece of formative assessment, but select a sample of work on which to provide formative assessment. When this technique has been used by the author a related strategy of getting students to consider previous feedback on each subsequent piece of formative assessment has been encouraged. This has the added benefit of getting students to think about their feedback and incorporate it as part of their learning through assessment.

A related technique in this vein is to provide feedback on a sub-set of student assessments and then get students to cascade the feedback as part of a peer feedback process.

One time-saving device is to make use of a rubric or feedback chart or grid – an example of mapping performance against learning outcome criteria is given in Chapter 3. The idea behind this technique is that you indicate the main learning outcomes on a pre-designed grid and then indicate the level of success that a student has attained as part of the feedback. This technique may save time, but is not necessarily particularly constructive unless it is accompanied by formative and developmental comments.

How many times have you written the same or similar comments when commenting on a set of assessment activities? Why not utilise this and develop a generic report indicating the common strengths and issues – again this technique can be enhanced by supplementing with individual comments.

Related to the generic comment approach is using a databank of common phrases. Here a series of common phrases and comments are held on a database and an individual feedback report is constructed from the comments. It is possible to contextualise this approach by embedding the databank comments in the body of the student assessment. This technique lends itself to automation.

Following on from the automated suggestion in the previous example – the use of computer-mediated programmes for production of feedback can be efficient and effective. Details of computer-mediated and Information and Communication Technologies approaches to formative assessment and formative feedback are addressed in more detail in Chapter 5.

EXAMPLES OF GOOD PRACTICE

Many of the techniques indicated as good practice can easily fall into the realms of 'not-so-good practice' if not used constructively. The simplest way to think about good practice is to think how the feedback provided will enhance student learning and understanding.

Close the gap

Indicate what students have done well but also what they could do to improve. Good feedback should attempt to acknowledge the progress students have made in their learning and understanding through the provision of constructive comments and indications of how they can improve their learning for the future (feedforward). Hall and Burke (2003: 10) suggest that if students 'know what to do to improve they can the "close the gap" between what they can do or know and what they need to do or know'. Hall and Burke go on to argue that 'it is better to focus on causes of success and failure than to praise performance on the basis of the final product or completed task'. The feedback should address complex learning issues, such as addressing quality of argument, completeness of discussion or interpretation of literature, rather than focus on simple feedback such as exceeding word count or spelling and grammar.

Formative feedback should endeavour to provide students with an indication of where they are in relation to achieving learning outcomes or standards, where they need to progress to and how they will be able to reach the expected level. In order for this to be effective the feedback should be based on understood goals (for the student) which the student believes are achievable and valuable. Feedback should be understandable and communicated in such a way as to enable students to use the feedback to help in achieving the learning outcomes or reaching the required standard.

Similarly, feedback should be worded in such a way as to encourage students to take actions to address any learning issues.

Providing formative feedback on summative assessment

We have already discussed the argument that students appear to be motivated by summative assessment. Until there is an appropriate culture change, which sees a reduction in the amount of summative assessment and a change in student motivation to be driven by learning opportunities (such as formative assessment, reflective learning and independent learning), summative assessment would seem to be a major factor in the student learning experience. Given that we have to deal with summative assessment, then we should aim to provide high quality, timely, formative feedback on summative assessment that will help students in their learning and help in 'bridging the gap' between where they are at the time of submitting the summative assessment and where they would hope to be to meet appropriate criteria and standards.

Making effective use of ICTs in formative assessment and formative feedback

There have been tremendous strides forward in educational technology over the last few years, and although there is debate as to the real impact of this technology on learning and teaching there are opportunities to make use of the technology in formative activities, both in terms of formative assessment and in the creation of timely formative feedback. Using ICTs may well be one of the ways to address the workload demands in our mass education systems and the investment in time and effort to develop your ICT usage may well reap benefits later on. The use of ICTs will be discussed in detail in Chapter 5.

Use of model solutions

Although many tutors do not feel comfortable in making use of this technique it can be a very positive approach. It is a particularly powerful approach when students are given indications of how their response differed from the model solution, and are given an indication of how they arrived at the different solution and why their approach is not as appropriate as the model solution. Alternatively, students could have found a 'better' or 'equally valid alternate' approach or answer and this allows for praise and congratulation.

There is a potential danger that this is not a particularly useful approach because it is possible that, without guidance on how to use the model solution in their learning, students will not deconstruct the model answer and they may decide that any work they have done which deviates from the model is wrong.

Use of model solutions as guidance and clarity before students tackle the exercise

Another way of making use of model solutions is to provide students with worked examples before they undertake assessment activities (either formative or summative). This approach can give students useful guidance on academic expectations, standards and possible approaches. However, there are potential downsides to this approach, either that students think the model solution is the only way to tackle the task, or that you need to provide many different exemplars in order to cover all possible approaches!

Getting students to think about feedback in advance

The SENLEF Project (2004) (see Juwah *et al.*, 2004) suggests that a constructive way of reducing academic workload and helping to provide feedback that students will value is to get students to determine the type of feedback they would like, by getting students to either:

- suggest the feedback they would like when they submit an assessment; or
- identify the difficulties they have had when they hand in assessments, and giving feedback focused on these difficulties.

Using this approach will encourage students to think about their assessment activity (and learn from the assessment activity), develop skills in self-assessment and self-awareness, and encourage them to make positive use of the feedback they receive (written and through dialogue).

The approach also potentially cuts down elements of the academic workload, but has the downside of possibly missing a major issue. By not discussing a major flaw in the student's work (assuming it is there) the student will possibly assume that the flaw does not exist.

Multiple Choice Questions (MCQs)

MCQs can be a very helpful and constructive tool for formative assessment and in the provision of formative feedback, but it is important to take great care in the design of questions. The MCQ approach lends itself very nicely to the use of ICTs such as QuestionMark or quizzes in Blackboard. In terms of feedback it is suggested that in order make constructive use of MCQs it is beneficial to:

- indicate to students why the answer they have selected was correct and why the other answers weren't correct;
- indicate the type of error or mistake the student could have made in reaching the incorrect answer;
- always using positive and supportive language.

Integrating formative activities into teaching practice

There are many opportunities to provide formative interventions and immediate feedback in a range of teaching situations (irrespective of class size) – examples given here focus on lecture sessions and practical classes but formative interventions and dialogue can take place in a whole range of teaching situations.

 Teaching Tip

It is worth telling students that feedback is actually taking place! This is not intended to be patronising, but it would appear that often students are not aware that interventions can actually be feedback!

Lecture sessions – formative assessment and formative feedback are possible in lectures by encouraging students to participate in learning activities in the lecture session. Interaction between the lecturer and students in lecture sessions helps develop rapport and 'breaks up' the session into smaller 'chunks' thus giving consideration to the attention span of students. Interaction can be instigated by lecturer questions, small group tasks, tasks specified in lecture handouts or checking for understanding. Dialogue in lectures provides an opportunity to give feedback to the whole student cohort. Interaction of this sort allows time for what Bligh (1998) refers to as 'information absorption'. Clarke *et al.* (2004: 259) suggest that using formative feedback reinforces the content of lectures and can act to 'cement students' understanding of key concepts and ideas'.

Practical sessions – a particularly powerful technique when having a tutor–student dialogue during a practical session is getting the student to explain why they have done a task a certain way. Formative assessment activities in practical situations can be designed to encourage students to discuss what they are doing, explain why they are doing it and justify any planned

77

course of action. The dialogue can be with a peer group or with a tutor, although the type of feedback could be different. Often when explaining practical activities student learning will take place through the process of developing the explanation for others. Peers and tutors can enhance the experience through dialogue by asking for clarification or justification but also by putting forward alternative solutions or options. According to Pelligrino *et al.* (2001: 85) 'practice is not enough to ensure that a skill will be acquired'. In order to acquire appropriate practical skills, students need to 'receive feedback about the correctness of what they have done'. When students make mistakes in practicals they need to understand the nature of their mistake and any mistakes can be explained through discussion and feedback.

Comments on draft coursework

Provide comments on draft coursework before submitting coursework for summative assessment. While this approach provides a very positive opportunity for formative feedback and student development of learning it is also potentially contentious and goes against custom and practice adopted at the author's institution. While there is potential benefit in providing feedback on summative coursework, there is also the potential for the standard of assessment to be perceived more along the lines of the NVQ approach to assessment. Similarly, there is a fine line between constructive, formative feedback and the lecturer providing 'too much' guidance to the extent that the work is not wholly the student's own. The level of formative support and feedback becomes potentially more 'grey' in supervision of projects and dissertations. An example of this approach is provided from Durham University in the case studies chapter.

Feedback on examinations

In theory, providing formative feedback on examination scripts should be no different from providing formative feedback on any other type of assessment mechanism. Students should be encouraged to learn from the examination assessment in the same way that they should be encouraged to learn from every assessment exercise. Providing feedback on examinations is often seen to be a contentious issue both from a university regulatory point of view and from a pragmatic timing perspective – for example:

- many universities have regulations which do not encourage students to have sight of their examination scripts;
- there are constraints such as the principle of double-blind marking – discourages writing on scripts; and
- the timing of examinations at the end of modules and at the end of the academic year.

While it would be beneficial to provide individualised feedback on examinations a more workable solution may be to provide general feedback on questions or subject areas as part of an oral group feedback session – which gets round potential regulatory hurdles and allows dialogue on examination performance. If examinations are set at the end of the module, then a constructive type of formative assessment and formative feedback is to get students to do 'mock exam' questions or work through past papers earlier on in the module schedule.

Encouraging self- and peer-assessment

Using self- and peer-assessment can be a very productive way to encourage engagement with formative activities and can help students learn from their assessment and their feedback. As has already been observed, developing skills in self-assessment will help students in their reflective practice and their self-development but will also help them understand their assessment and feedback from other sources. Research, such as that undertaken by McDonald and Boud (2003), indicates that encouraging students to participate in self-assessment and engage in reflecting on their own learning goals is 'highly effective in enhancing learning and achievement'. Students will benefit from the feedback that we provide if they have developed skills in self-assessment and peer-assessment. Self- and peer-assessment will also provide an alternative set of student learning opportunities.

Falchikov (2004) suggests that students can be involved in assessment in three distinct areas – namely traditional (and non-traditional) academic activity, performance in academic settings and professional practices. In deciding how to utilise peer-assessment you need to consider the ways in which you wish your students to contribute, remembering that the outcomes from academic activities are products, while for performance in academic settings and professional practices the outcomes are processes.

Peer-assessment can be constructive and helpful in encouraging dialogue but also help in getting students to understand the assessment activities, learn from the assessment and develop constructive and valuable feedback.

79

Self- and peer-assessment can also save a significant amount of academic staff time in the provision of feedback, although the reduction of staff workload should not be used as a primary justification for the inclusion or use of self- and peer-assessment. A case study on peer-assessment, from the University of Queensland, is provided in Chapter 7.

There are potential concerns for students about using peer- and self-assessment – such as:

- worry that that they are doing the teacher's job for them;
- concern that they don't have the subject knowledge to give feedback;
- understanding assessment criteria and expectations;
- concern that they don't have the pedagogic abilities to be constructive and supportive in providing feedback;
- potential bias in giving feedback (friendships/animosities/competition); or
- fear of being critical to their peers.

But with discussion, clear guidance, support and the development of assessment skills these concerns can be overcome. A little bit of investment in time and effort in getting your students to be able and comfortable with peer- and self-assessment can improve self- and peer-assessment but can also help their understanding of the assessment process and the formative feedback that you give them as part of tutor assessment.

If you wish to consider using self- and peer-evaluation in your formative activities you are recommended to look at the work undertaken by Boud (1989), Sambell *et al.* (1999), Sluijsmans *et al.* (2001), McDonald and Boud (2003) and Falchikov (2005) for guidance and suggestions for good practice.

 Time Out

▶ How could you utilise self- and peer-assessment in your teaching?

▶ What guidance do you think you would need to give your students?

▶ How can you encourage students to engage in the process and get them to see the value of the process?

Portfolios

Portfolios are a very useful mechanism for providing formative feedback, particularly when used to engage students in a process of self-reflective learning. Portfolios can be used to encourage dialogue – by getting students to talk about their portfolio entries and provide a rationale for the work they have provided in their portfolios, either in tutorials, peer evaluation or presentations. Baume (2001) advocates that portfolios are a 'valid, reliable, fair and economical' means of assessment, and goes on to suggest that portfolios 'stimulate students to produce work which they value', 'safely stretch and challenge students', 'lead to students doing things which lead directly to learning', and 'help students to know the extent and the limits of what they know'. The points made by Baume on portfolios encapsulate many of the principles of formative assessment and formative feedback. Irons (2002) found that 'the experience of students constructing portfolios has indicated that there is opportunity for regular formative feedback as the portfolio develops'.

Feedback sheets using criteria

Using feedback sheets (linked to learning outcomes or assessment objectives) can be a fast and effective way of providing formative feedback as long as they are carefully designed and utilised in such a way as to give students constructive feedback. They can be used to indicate to students the parts of an activity they did well and the parts they didn't do so well. It is important to supplement 'tick box' type feedback with some written and individualised comments. The benefit to academics is that the method can be fast (although it can take quite a deal of effort to set up in the first place – so size of student cohort and opportunities for reusability are important to consider) and can avoid the situation of having to write out the same comments on the work of every student. Some authors, such as Sadler (1983), have suggested that the use of criteria promotes a tick-list approach to the activity (from the student perception) and potentially loses the opportunity for comment on the holistic nature of the formative assessment task.

Addressing assessment issues such as plagiarism

Plagiarism and other forms of academic misconduct or cheating would appear to be a growing issue in higher education (McDowell and Brown, 2001).

The development of the Internet as a resource and the use of Information and Communication Technology potentially makes academic misconduct easier for students. Guidelines for good practice on how to deal with plagiarism can be found in Carroll and Appleton (2001). Formative activities can be designed to address plagiarism and other forms of misconduct and students can be given feedback on academic standards and expectations in the 'safe' environment of formative assessment. It is possible to use ICT plagiarism detection tools to provide formative feedback for students – see chapter on use of ICTs.

 Time Out

▶ Which of these techniques would you use in your assessment activities:

a) in formative assessment?
b) in summative assessment?

▶ Would you use different techniques between formative and summative assessments?

If so why?
If not, why not?

EXAMPLES OF NOT-SO-GOOD PRACTICE

There are many situations where a lack of appropriate intervention, dialogue or support can be counterproductive to students' formative development. Problems can arise before students even start the formative assessment task, for example the task brief might not be clear or have sufficient guidance or students might not have experienced the type of task before – both situations meaning that students are not sure what is expected from them. The situation could arise where students are unable to discuss the task with tutors in order to obtain clarification.

However, the main focus in this section is to give examples of feedback practice which we should try to avoid either because the feedback fails to add any value, is confusing or ambiguous, is counterproductive or is demotivating for students.

No feedback

Perhaps the worst-case scenario and the most frustrating for students is if we don't give any feedback at all: then it is certainly the case that students will not learn anything from the feedback. However, the situation is worse than that. They will not necessarily learn from undertaking their actual assessment itself (not having their perceptions of learning confirmed). Not giving students any feedback will also potentially have an adverse impact on their motivation and will discourage students from participation in future assessments (either summative or formative).

Feedback that is not timely

Providing feedback that is not timely is nearly as damaging as providing no feedback at all. As discussed in Chapter 3, Cowan (2003) suggests that the most effective feedback is provided 'within minutes' of students completing a task (see Chapter 3 for discussions on unitisation, bunching of assessment, end-of-unit assessment and feedforward). Not providing feedback on time really upsets students, will probably have minimal impact on their learning (so all the work you put into giving the feedback is wasted time) and will almost certainly become an issue – and will be reflected in activities such as the National Student Survey and external reviews.

There is a potential issue in terms of balancing the quality and quantity of feedback with the pressures of time and workload. This is an example of where working with students in terms of indicating when feedback will be given, discussing the type of feedback (perhaps explaining why it takes time), focusing on specific points in feedback or working on a strategy of self- or peer-assessment can alleviate some of the issues.

Numeric mark only

Butler (1988) argues that students pay less attention to tutor comments and formative feedback when they are given a numeric mark for assessments. As a result the students focus on the numeric mark, often using it as a means of comparison with their peers, and do not try to use the formative feedback to bridge the gap(s) in their learning or understanding. Craven *et al.* (1991) found that feedback given in numeric form has an 'especially negative effect on the self-esteem of low ability students'. Black (1999) argues that the best approach in formative feedback is not to use numeric indicators at all.

There are a number of strategies to address this:

1) Don't give a numeric mark at all – can drift in to being counter-productive as students often want this.
2) Give numeric mark at a later date than the written or verbal feedback.
3) Give numeric mark only after students have shown evidence of reflecting on the written or verbal feedback you have provided (could be written reflection or outcome of dialogue).

Contradictory feedback

Giving students a comment of 'good work' (not in itself particularly helpful, although it can act as a motivator) and giving a numeric mark of 35 per cent. It is confusing for students and does not help them to appreciate how they have performed against a specific task, or help them to understand how to close the gap in their learning.

Lack of consistency of feedback between lecturers

In some sense a similar issue to contradictory feedback, in that it can give confusing messages to students (particularly when student-to-student dialogue is encouraged). Lack of consistency can manifest itself as a problem, either when a range of tutors are providing feedback on one piece of work (which should be picked up during moderation, but this is not always the case) or between different modules on the same programme (the discussion about student expectation has been addressed in Chapter 1).

Unhelpful feedback

Unhelpful feedback can take a range of formats and we should make every effort not to provide feedback that will be counterproductive. One of the worst forms of unhelpful feedback is feedback that is overly critical of student work (being overly critical serves no constructive purpose and can be very demotivating for students).

Chamberlain *et al.* (1998) give a range of interesting examples of feedback that is unhelpful for students, which include unfocused comments

— these are comments that do not address learning needs or are ambiguous, or are so asinine that they do not help students in their understanding, for example making use of terms such as:

- 'confused'
- 'generally sound'
- 'adequate'
- 'careful how you begin your sentences'.

Chamberlain *et al.* (1998) also raise concerns about the dismissive use of sarcastic comments, such as:

- 'did you experiment to find all this?'
- 'most of this is straight from the book'.

These only serve to undermine student confidence and give no regard for the time and effort students have put into the activity. You might feel like writing these comments – but don't share them with students!

Another set of unhelpful comments are ones that 'pass the buck' or focus on simple issues such as spelling or grammar while ignoring the more difficult abstract learning requirements such as critical analysis, for example:

- 'you need help with your English'
- 'see an academic skills adviser'.

Comments sending mixed messages or unclear messages – the examples Chamberlain *et al.* (1998) suggest include comments such as:

- 'text is based on only a few readings and not on your own thinking'
- 'follow your own advice'.

 Time Out

▶ How would you react to feedback comments like these?

▶ How many times have you used these or something similar?

▶ Did your students learn anything from these comments?

SUMMARY

There are many techniques and methods for providing students with feedback. It is not the case that any one of these is always the best method for giving feedback and the type of feedback given will depend on the situation, the objective in providing feedback, the environment and the student.

It is also true to say that the various tools, techniques and methods discussed in this chapter should not necessarily be used in isolation and often a combination of different techniques will provide the most benefit for students in terms of enhancing their learning.

Great care needs to be taken in when, how and why we are providing feedback. As has been shown with the examples of 'not-so-good practice' it is not enough to provide feedback on its own — it has to be appropriate feedback which is constructive and helpful.

Chapter 5

Making use of ICTs in formative assessment and formative feedback

CHAPTER SUMMARY

This chapter will consider the use of Information and Communication Technologies in formative assessment and how ICTs allow for the provision of effective and efficient formative feedback. This chapter also examines methods and techniques for utilising ICTs in order to provide individualised, effective and timely feedback. The chapter illustrates that ICTs are not limited to numeric, mathematical or scientific exercises but can be used across a range of subject domains. In this chapter we will also discuss some of the issues associated with using ICT to provide the platform for formative activities and the potential issues related to changes in practice, workload, reliability of systems and student perceptions of using ICT.

INTRODUCTION

Today information technology seems to be all pervading. The uptake in new technologies is exceptionally fast and the development of new technologies to replace the current technologies is an ongoing evolution (and sometimes revolution). The other side of the coin is concern about the role of information technologies, the lack of robustness of technologies and the fact that technologies are quickly replaced. Both sides of the argument have an impact on the use of technology in education and the expectations of the stakeholders in education, for example, students, tutors, managers, the government and the public.

Using ICTs to facilitate formative activities should not be an end in itself but should be seen as a means to an end. In the context of formative assessment there are opportunities to provide a variety of formative assessment mechanisms and certainly the opportunity to provide formative assessment activities which students can choose to undertake when it suits them. In the context of formative feedback, using ICTs should be seen as a way of improving the quality of feedback and of speeding up the process of providing feedback. ICTs may also help in managing the workload issues alluded to in Chapters 2 and 3.

While we advocate the use of ICTs as being a benefit to higher education – there is also a cautionary warning that needs to be given. There is a danger that ICTs are seen as the panacea for many of the current issues in higher education, and may be viewed as a set of tools to resolve all the issues and challenges in formative assessment and formative feedback. We need to take great care in remembering that utilising ICTs in any aspect of education, including formative activities, requires a great deal of time, effort and development. Often this is required 'up front' before any real savings or efficiencies can be made. Using ICTs in formative assessment and formative feedback is not a cheap or easy option!

The focus of this chapter is to discuss the types of ICT tool which can be utilised in formative assessment and formative feedback and to examine the benefits (and potential pitfalls) of using ICT in formative activities. It is not the intention to go into all the detail associated with using ICT in teaching, or in the enhancement of teaching and learning; however, it is hoped that a discussion of the potential of ICT in formative activities may prove useful and help you decide on whether you would want to utilise ICTs in your professional practice and in what circumstances you might choose to use ICT.

ICT in higher education has been around for a long time – from the Flowers Report (1965), progressing to the Dearing Report (1997) (see NCIHE, 1997), through the Joint Information Systems Committee (JISC) initiative (1999) and culminating in the 2003 White Paper, which suggests that e-learning should be embedded in 'a full and sustainable way by 2013', (HEFCE, 2003: 64). The stated goal of the Higher Education Funding Council for England (HEFCE) in the recently published e-learning strategy is to 'help the sector use new technology as effectively as they can, so that it becomes a "normal" or embedded part of their activities' (HEFCE, 2005).

There have been many initiatives, national and local, in the intervening period aiming to address the integration of ICT into HE teaching (and research). Initiatives include the Computers in Teaching Initiative (CTI) (which operated from 1985 to 1999 and was superseded by the Learning and Teaching Support Network (LTSN), which were subsequently integrated into the Higher Education Academy in 2004), the Teaching and

Learning Technology Programme (TLTP) phases 1, 2 and 3, and Fund for the Development of Learning and Teaching (FDTL), phases 1, 2, 3 and 4. These national initiatives, alongside local activities, were designed to embed the use of ICT into teaching (and research) in HE.

The government (White Paper and other HEFCE documents), educational managers (Ramsden, 1998), advocates (Conole and Oliver, 1998; Collis and Moonen, 2001; Laurillard, 2002; Salmon, 2000, 2002; Jochems *et al.*, 2004) and commercial organisations (WebCT and Blackboard, for example) all enthuse about the use of ICTs and e-learning and the opportunities afforded by exploiting the potential of educational technologies and e-learning. Ramsden (1992: 5) argues that technology is helping change the nature of university teaching as a method for imparting knowledge to an environment that 'makes student learning possible'. However, George (2002) cautions that 'IT is an enabler, not a solution in itself' and McGettrick *et al.* (2004) suggest that 'despite advances that are being made in relation to its uptake, there are many who strongly believe that the effectiveness of e-learning remains one of the "grand challenges" for education in the coming decades'.

National strategies and policies for the HE sector, and in particular the role of ICT to support learning, teaching and research, sit within a context of rapid technological change (Conole, 2001). Educational technology and tools to support e-learning are part of the environment in HE and in many ways contribute to the challenge of the traditional teaching functions of the HE sector – and this is certainly the case in formative assessment and formative feedback.

ICT adoption in universities is not necessarily the answer to all the issues in HE but can contribute to facing the challenges of rising student numbers, reduction in finance, ICT expectation of graduates seeking employment and society's expectation of value from HE.

Brown *et al.* (1999) suggest three benefits that have been demonstrated in using ICTs for assessment:

- reducing the load on teachers by automating appropriate parts of the task of marking students' work;
- providing students with detailed formative feedback on their learning much more efficiently than is usually possible with traditional assessment;
- bringing the assessment culture experienced by students closer to the (computer based) learning environments with which they are increasingly familiar and confident.

There are many reasons for using ICTs in formative assessment and formative feedback, for ICTs will:

- Support the changing and increasingly diverse student population – for example, there are more students having to work to support their studies, more part-time students, more students from different backgrounds (see the discussion on student experience in Chapter 1).
- Tackle the issue of increasing staff student ratio.
- Provide greater flexibility and choice for students.
- Provide automated responses to formative activities.
- Speed up the provision of feedback – either through automated responses (e.g. multiple choice questions) or through providing generic feedback or making use of ICT for speedier communication (e.g. e-mail).
- Allow students to use online discussion fora for peer-assessment and evaluation.
- Link to government policy (e.g. NCIHE (1997) recommends 'computer based programmes such as tutorials . . . can be highly interactive and provide activities that students need to develop their understanding of others' ideas and the articulation of their own').

ICT APPLICATION AND WORKLOAD

Throughout the evolution of educational technology and e-learning very little time or effort have been given to examining the effect of using ICT or the demands e-learning make on teachers in HE. Research that has been undertaken on the impact of technology tends to focus on the secondary school sector and on the adoption and usage of ICTs (using metrics such as ratio of student to computer or the implementation of a physical infrastructure) or the lack of change in teaching practice as a result of ICT implementation (Cuban *et al.*, 2001; Curran, 2001; Pelgrum, 2001) – suggesting traditional approach but using ICTs.

A review of the literature indicates that very little research has been undertaken on the actual impact on teachers in terms of workload, skills development (pedagogic and technical), changes in teaching practice, or enhancement of student learning.

There is a general perception that the use of educational technology and e-learning makes teaching in HE more efficient and enhances the student experience (summarised by Masi and Winer (2005: 150), indicating that there is an 'intuitive sense that what teachers and students can do with technology is 'better' than what can be done without it'), but this assertion is made without giving adequate consideration to what the implications are for teachers in HE.

 Time Out

▶ Why are we using e-learning to support learning and teaching?

▶ To what extent does technology provide an effective vehicle for good teaching?

▶ How can e-learning be used effectively and efficiently to enhance learning and teaching? (And how can teachers in HE evaluate/know this?)

▶ What measurements can be used to analyse teaching before the introduction of e-learning and after the introduction of e-learning?

▶ What evidence might teachers cite to justify their belief in e-learning?

▶ How are staff empowered in order to engage with e-learning?

▶ What strategic decisions/directions do HE institutions need to take, particularly in terms of change management associated with e-learning?

▶ Is the student perception of good teaching the same as academic staff perception of good teaching?

There is a need for academic staff to invest time in developing the appropriate technical and pedagogic skills required to make best use of ICTs. Similarly, there is a need for a robust technical infrastructure to support the use of ICTs.

ICTs can reduce the workload for academic staff and potentially remove some of the constraints that make formative assessment and formative feedback impractical. ICTs can be used to act as an automated tutor in order to extract features of student responses and analyse those responses to identify errors and provide feedback for correcting those errors.

MAKING USE OF ICTS IN FORMATIVE ASSESSMENT AND FORMATIVE FEEDBACK

The use of ICTs in formative assessment (sometimes referred to as e-assessment) allows for the provision of effective and efficient feedback that can be individualised, allows for student interaction and is provided in a timely manner. Charman (1999) argues that ICTs 'could engage students even if there was no summative element involved' and that 'there is mounting evidence for the pedagogic advantages of CBA [computer based assessment] in providing feedback on student work in higher education'. ICTs are not limited to numeric, mathematical or scientific exercises, but can be used across a range of subject domains. When ICTs are used in formative assessment and formative feedback, academic staff should be aware of the need to consider students' perception of ICTs and their skills and abilities in using ICTs. Laurillard (2002) advocates the need to use appropriate pedagogy in the use of ICTs in learning and teaching, and it is certainly the case that pedagogic considerations require to be taken into account in the use of ICTs in formative assessment and feedback.

Brosnan (1999) discusses the concept of 'computer anxiety' as a drawback for the use of ICTs in formative assessment, although Bull and Stevens (1999) concluded that 'very few students were fearful of having to use computers to perform assessments'. On the other hand Sambell *et al.* (1999: 183) discovered that the majority of students found computer based tests less stressful than traditional examinations. It is worthwhile, when considering the use of ICTs in formative assessment, to think about the impact using ICTs might have on the activity!

Utilising ICTs in formative activities can provide a number of pedagogic benefits for students, including:

- improved flexibility, in that students can participate at their own pace and undertake the activities when they want to and even undertake the formative activities on multiple occasions;
- adaptive testing can be used in order to match the formative assessment to individual students' ability;
- automated and immediate feedback (see Denton, 2001);
- the opportunity to monitor their own progress and development;
- the opportunity for students to participate in formative dialogue (Boud and Knights, 1994; Lea, 2001).

In addition, academic staff can utilise automated formative assessment tools to:

- monitor student levels of participation;
- guide students in their learning by providing clues and tips;
- reduce the time spent on marking (after initial investment of time and effort); and
- produce diagnostic reports and individualised feedback.

EXAMPLES OF ICT USAGE IN FORMATIVE ASSESSMENT AND FORMATIVE FEEDBACK

The following examples illustrate some of the possibilities for ICT usage in formative assessment and feedback.

Virtual Learning Environments (VLEs) such as Blackboard, WebCT or Moodle

VLEs provide a number of features which can be used to provide effective formative assessment and formative feedback, for example the use of announcements, quizzes (see discussion on effective use of multiple choice questionnaires), online discussions (useful for peer-assessment) and the academic's summary of those online discussions.

VLEs provide opportunity for communication and dialogue between tutors and students and between students – the online discussion boards and the virtual seminar facilities in products such as Blackboard are very popular with students. We do need to take care in the use of this technology to:

a) ensure that all students have appropriate access to the technology and are comfortable in using it;
b) ensure that we have the appropriate technical and pedagogical skills to facilitate learning using VLEs.

If you intend to use a VLE (your institution may have invested heavily in a VLE and you may be expected to use it) then you need to be sure that the VLE is robust and stable, and is accessible by students at times when the students want to access it (in effect this means 24/7 access). You may find tensions arise between academic staff and technical staff if the VLE is not as robust as it needs to be, or tensions between academic staff and administrative staff develop if students do not have access to the modules and programmes that they expect to have.

The majority of academics have progressed through an education system without experience of VLEs from a student perspective and it is suggested that we would all benefit in our teaching and the provision of online formative feedback if we experienced the VLE from a student perspective.

E-mail

E-mail can be an effective (and simple) means of communicating formative feedback to students, either on an individualised basis (for example using statement banks, see below) or for generic issues relevant to the whole student cohort on a module.

The use of e-mail as a means of supporting students can lead to an interesting pedagogical change in the role of the tutor. Grandgenett and Grandgenett (2001) suggest a five-step approach to tutors using e-mail to resolve student problems and go on to indicate that there is a specific art to e-mail support. Students need to be convinced of the better learning opportunity in support via e-mail and there is a potential danger of non-participation from students if they do not see the benefits.

E-mail is not the only ICT facility with which there is potential non-participation from students. An example taken from the author's experience illustrates one of the pedagogical issues faced in using ICTs. Simply giving students access to online formative exercises does not mean that they will participate in the activities. As we have seen in Chapter 2, there is an expectation that students obtain a reward (mainly summative marks) in undertaking work.

Holt *et al.* (2002) report in their survey on using web-based support for campus-based open learning that 'online discussions did not work well', claiming that part of the reason for lack of participation was due to student choice because of 'the fact that contributions to discussion boards were unassessed, and thus viewed as optional'. However, Holt *et al.* (2002) go on to argue that students did not participate or make use of online learning because 'they felt that online discussion was inferior to face-to-face exchanges', and that 'it was simply easier and better to resolve issues when they met [student and tutor]'.

Plagiarism Advisory Service

While the Plagiarism Advisory Service has been designed primarily to help students appreciate the level of originality of their work, and identify situations where there may be problems with academic misconduct before submitting work for summative assessment, it can be a very positive tool in the provision of formative feedback, particularly when it is used to help educate students about the need for, and mechanics of, accurate referencing and citation. The 'originality reports' produced by the Turnitin® UK software will not only demonstrate where citation has been inadequate, but will also indicate if particular types of resources are causing problems for the individual student. In addition, the visual elements of the report clearly highlight where 'patch writing' has occurred, and thereby provide an opportunity for both student and lecturer to discuss the require-ments of academic writing in a constructive and timely manner. Utilising detection software tools in formative assignments can help to redress the problems of inadequate referencing and citation before bad practice becomes entrenched.

The service is available at www.unn.ac.uk/central/isd/PDS.htm.

Personal Response System

ICTs can be used in the classroom for instant feedback, for example using the Personal Response System (PRS). Students are given handsets and are asked to respond to questions (normally embedded in a PowerPoint presentation). The PRS is a teaching method that involves interaction between the lecturer and a group of students in a live, lecture-based situa-tion (such as the 'ask the audience' in 'Who Wants to be a Millionaire™', copyright © Celador). Students can be posed formative questions that are presented within a PowerPoint presentation. Students are then asked to answer the question electronically, using a small handheld transmitter to register a response.

The lecturer can examine the nature of student responses to assess student comprehension and use the analysis in a number of ways, e.g. inform future teaching sessions, guide directed learning activity, influence nature of student project work.

Students may also want to analyse accuracy of response, which may then inform revision activity or other independent learning activity. Having used this technology, it certainly helps keep the lecturer on their toes, because often the feedback is not as one would expect or predict!

Automated formative feedback tools

There are a number of commercial packages which support the auto-mated delivery of formative feedback, such as Questionmark, WebMCQ, Examine and EQL Assessor. Some packages, such as Formative Automated

Computer Testing (FACT) (see Hunt *et al.* (2002)), are specifically designed to provide formative feedback.

QuestionMark Perception is an ICT product which allows academics to author, administer, deliver and report on computerised assessments. QuestionMark Perception is available for web delivery and Windows® delivery. The package allows for formative feedback to be given to students at item, topic and/or assessment levels. Feedback can also include hyperlinks to appropriate learning materials and web-based applications. Bull and Stevens (1999) discuss the benefits of using QuestionMark in both summative and formative assessment. Full details about QuestionMark are available at www.questionmark.com.

Database of question/response banks

ICTs can be used to facilitate the use of question banks, useful in the generation of formative activities and in the use of question response banks. Question response banks can be used to generate 'individualised' formative feedback through the extraction of text from the response bank dependent on the 'keys' the assessor uses in generating the response.

Utilising electronic whiteboards

Making use of electronic whiteboards can be a very effective means of providing immediate formative feedback on student work or additional formative feedback on material that you are using in your teaching.

Normally, when electronic whiteboards are used, a presentation is the focal point for discussion and dialogue. This can take the form of a student presentation and can be presented as a word-processor document, a design diagram, a map or a worked example. Indeed, it can be anything that you might want to discuss or annotate.

There are many ways to utilise this technology in the provision of formative feedback, but one example is to take a presentation and display it on the board and then annotate the presentation as the discussion progresses. The annotated version can then be saved as a record of the formative activity and copies either printed or e-mailed to students for future reference.

SUMMARY

There are many positive opportunities in the use of ICTs, which can be utilised in the provision of formative assessment and formative feedback.

There is a very positive opportunity to provide immediate feedback, which will hopefully help student learning and address many of the issues of timeliness of feedback (of course there is a need to have quality feedback as well as timely feedback and we should not forget this in our use of ICTs – the rubbish-in, rubbish-out analogy can be applied to educational ICT usage in the same way as it can be applied to all IT systems).

We need to remember that ICTs are not a quick or easy solution to the problems in higher education – but with appropriate time, appropriate technical and pedagogical skills and a robust IT infrastructure there are opportunities to embrace the technology to enhance student learning.

Chapter 6

Benefits of formative feedback for academic staff

CHAPTER SUMMARY

Formative feedback is not only an activity aimed at student learning, but can be used as a contribution to the evaluation of activities and as an input to staff development. This chapter will consider the benefits of reflecting on how students respond to formative assessment and formative feedback and how to make use of the opportunity to consider the effectiveness of the teaching and learning methods and techniques that have been used. The process of interpreting student perception and understanding of formative activities can provide a substantiated rationale for modifying teaching activities and practices. This chapter seeks to identify the student interactions that can benefit academic staff, to illustrate ways in which to gather and analyse the information and discuss how that information can be used to reinforce good practice or as a rationale for changing existing practice. The chapter will also give consideration as to how academic staff can learn about and develop their teaching practice by obtaining their own formative feedback through activities such as peer observation and mentoring.

INTRODUCTION

Making use of formative assessment and formative feedback can be an interesting and informative way to reflect on, and ultimately enhance, your teaching. In Black and Wiliam's (1998) discussion on formative assessment they suggest that one of the outcomes from formative activities is that it is used to 'adapt the teaching work to meet the needs'. Black and Wiliam (1998) take the point further in suggesting that formative assessment includes 'all those activities undertaken by teachers and by their students assessing themselves, which provide information to be used as feedback to modify the teaching and learning activities in which they are based'. Applying Black and Wiliam's suggestion means formative feedback can lead to an immediate change in teaching or be considered in the longer term for module or programme change.

Feedback can be obtained from sources internal to your institution including students, peers, critical friends or mentors and can be done formally or informally. Alternatively, feedback may be obtained from third parties external to your institution such as external examiners (not particularly likely in practice), professional bodies or the Quality Assurance Agency. These types of interaction can provide a rich source of data which can be used to reflect on your practice.

Getting feedback from your students can be a really useful technique in helping you to evaluate and shape your teaching and providing you with an indication of formative activities which are effective and enhance learning, or methods that students engage with and value, or indeed providing you with an indication of areas where students are finding difficulty – this could be at a subject level or indeed at a technique level.

Reflecting on how students respond to formative feedback affords the opportunity to consider the effectiveness of the teaching and learning methods and the techniques employed in formative assessment, and the effectiveness of the formative feedback provided. The interpretation of student perception and understanding of formative activities provides a substantiated rationale for modifying activities and practice.

TEACHERS LEARNING FROM ASSESSMENT

Yorke (2003: 482) suggests that the 'act of assessing has an effect on the assessor as well as the student. Assessors learn about the extent to which the students have developed expertise and can tailor their teaching accordingly'. Reflecting on how students respond to formative assessment and formative feedback provides the opportunity to consider the effectiveness of the teaching and learning methods and techniques being employed. Interpretation of student perception and understanding of formative activities provides a substantiated rationale for modifying activities and practice.

There are many opportunities to adjust your teaching in order to take into account the results of assessment (formative and summative). Depending on the type of assessment and the timing of the assessment this could mean a change to the teaching scheme in a module, with more time spent on areas students are having problems with (care needs to be taken to ensure coverage of whole syllabus), or be used as useful input to module review, with changes taking place in the next iteration of the module (having gone through the normal quality assurance processes and procedures).

Formative assessment can provide information for academics on the subject areas that students find difficult or are experiencing difficulties with. This in turn can provide information on where to focus teaching efforts or to review the particular teaching techniques used in that subject area.

There are many ways to determine the subjects that students are having difficulty in grasping. One of the key opportunities is in the generation of feedback – if you find you are providing similar feedback to many students (one way of cutting down workload is to utilise generic responses – see Chapter 4), then it may well be an indicator for you that students have either not understood the subject that the assessment pertains to or perhaps that the assessment task was not particularly clear (perhaps in language or in level of guidance).

ACADEMIC MOTIVATION

There are many different reasons that motivate people to work in higher education, including teaching, consultancy and research – and to be honest probably a mix of all three. It is not the intention in this book to question the role of higher education, but it is worth thinking about what the motivation is for providing formative assessment opportunities and giving students feedback. In section 4.1 of the 2003 White Paper on Higher Education it is suggested that 'all students are entitled to be taught well, and to be given the support they need to learn effectively'. As has been shown in Chapters 1 and 2, giving students feedback on their work helps in developing student learning.

 Time Out

▶ Why have you chosen a career in higher education?

▶ What aspects of your job give you the most satisfaction?

▶ Where do student learning and student achievement rank in your priorities?

▶ How do you think utilisation of formative activities can help your job satisfaction?

Incorporation of formative assessment and formative feedback can make teaching more rewarding and satisfying, especially when student learning is enhanced and the results of formative activities lead to students developing their subject knowledge and their academic skills.

It is important that we take time to consider the quality of the feedback we provide and how that feedback helps students to learn from their assessment activities.

FEEDBACK ON TEACHING PRACTICE

There are a number of ways that we can use the principles of formative assessment and formative feedback as a means of gathering data on our teaching practice. This data can then be used as input to our reflective development and lead to enhancement of teaching. Techniques such as:

- feedback from students
- peer observation
- mentoring, and
- external review.

If the above methods are used sensitively and carefully, they can be very productive in providing effective feedback which can be used to enhance teaching practice. As with the discussion in Chapter 3 on engaging in dialogue between teachers and students, by getting teachers to discuss feedback with students, peers or mentors, learning from the feedback will be more effective. These methods don't happen as a matter of course and it is important to provide appropriate staff development and training, and ensure that all participants are comfortable with the rationale and objectives associated with the various exercises. It is suggested that obtaining feedback is much more constructive when it is seen as a personal development exercise as opposed to a management or regulatory or quality assurance exercise.

By letting your students see that you engage in obtaining feedback as part of your professional development, learning from that feedback and changing your teaching practice as a result, you will encourage students to appreciate the value of feedback. Swing (2004) argues that by acting as a role model, indicating your own demand for feedback and willingness to seek external feedback, the students will undertake a similar process. It is hoped that exposing students to a culture of giving and receiving feedback and acting on that feedback will help them to see the value in participating in the feedback process and enter into dialogue based on the feedback.

FEEDBACK FROM STUDENTS

A fairly obvious source of feedback that you can make use of in your reflection on teaching practice is from your students. It has been argued (Davidovitch and Soen, 2006) that student evaluations of teachers are highly reliable in that they 'correlate with other students on the same course and with retrospective evaluations of alumni'. Attempting to get feedback from your students conveys a commitment to professional development and improvement and also encourages students to think about their learning and teaching experiences. There may be contractual or regulatory reasons for obtaining student feedback. In the spirit of this book we suggest that feedback from students can be used in a formative and developmental way in order to encourage reflection and enhance teaching practice.

Prosser (2005) argues that data from students' surveys of the quality of teaching should take account of why different students experience their studies in different ways. We need to understand why students respond as they do during any given survey, and then take appropriate action in light of this understanding. This allows us to make changes that fully take account of this diverse range of students, and how their experiences, both past and present, relate to their perceptions of the quality of their educational experience.

It is important to note that such understanding will relate not simply to the quality of the teaching itself, but also to how students experience that teaching. For instance, students might perceive that the feedback they receive from lecturers is inadequate; however, this could be either because they do not appreciate the feedback that they do receive, or because the feedback is not adequate. We can thus focus any action either on helping our students to value the teaching that they receive or on the quality of the teaching itself.

We need to take into account a range of factors which might influence student feedback such as:

- learning environment (learning resources, time the class meets, class size, etc.);
- student motivation;
- reasons students have for taking a module;
- perceived difficulty or relevance of subject; or
- level of study and teacher experience.

There are a number of mechanisms that can be used to obtain feedback from students; these can be anonymous or not and formal or informal, and may or may not make use of ICTs. Instruments such as the National Student Survey and the Student Written Statement in quality assurance review as well as student input to professional body review provide formal opportunities for student input to the quality assurance process, and the processes of reflecting on learning and teaching.

Student feedback may be obtained at module or programme level (normally at each level as part of annual review rather than for the course of a whole programme). You may also be expected to get some form of individual feedback as part of your institution's regulations or it may even be a contractual obligation or expectation that you obtain student feedback on your teaching. This is normally undertaken as part of a formal process of review.

There are of course more informal methods for obtaining student feedback through discussion and dialogue in a variety of settings, including:

- Teaching situations – in the actual classroom or lecture room – for example getting students to write down what they have learned in a lecture session or perhaps what issues they expected to be addressed but haven't been.
- Discussions with groups of students – for example getting students to agree on what the key issues are in a particular topic are or getting them as a group to agree on what question(s) might be worth asking.
- Individual conversations – where we can address issues of expectation, understanding and enjoyment of the subject and of our teaching.

In deciding what approach to use in obtaining feedback you need to consider what you want the feedback for and what you are going to do as a result of getting the feedback.

We also need to take care not to sicken students with requests for feedback – feedback fatigue or questionnaire fatigue may set in with some students and as a result the quality of the feedback may be compromised.

PEER OBSERVATION

The process of peer observation is a method where a colleague provides feedback on your teaching with the objective of helping you to improve your teaching practice. It is suggested in this book that it is important that this is undertaken as a formative activity and is not seen as a tool for academic managers to make judgements on the quality of teaching. The principles of dialogue discussed in Chapter 2 are pertinent to the peer observation process.

It is suggested that there is discussion before and after the peer observation. The discussion before sets the 'goalposts' for the session and allows for negotiation on what the observer will focus on, possibly on areas where the colleague to be observed has concerns (possibly obtained from student feedback). Similarly, the discussion afterwards will allow for discussion about what went well in the session, where there may be room for improvement, including areas that were identified in the pre-observation discussion.

Peer observation can be helpful in identifying areas for improvement but also as a means of giving reassurance through giving positive feedback. Often the observer will identify a positive attribute that the observed person did not even realise was a positive attribute!

It is possible to use the peer observation process to examine specific issues or circumstances – such as providing feedback on a particular teaching innovation or in getting the observer to look for specific characteristics, attributes or interventions. For example, on one particular set of peer observations the author asked the observer to note the gender and ethnic origin of students every time he interacted with the student body. Over a period of observations a pattern of tending to interact with white male students was noted. The author was able to amend his teaching practice, and as a result planned his interactions to be more inclusive.

It is often the case that the person who benefits most from the process of peer observation is the observer – both from the actual observation and the pre and post discussions.

MENTORING

Many institutions are making use of mentoring as a means of staff development and the mentoring process can be a valuable source of formative feedback. New academic staff, probationary staff and staff promoted to new positions are often offered support from a mentor. In the author's institution all teaching staff are encouraged to have a mentor. The role of the mentor is intended to provide support to the 'mentee' (i.e. the person being mentored), normally on a one-to-one basis and in a confidential and 'safe' environment. The mentor can provide support and guidance on pragmatic aspects of the job such as teaching, research, contact with students and institutional bureaucracy and administration as well as guidance on career development. Normally, the mentor is a different person from the mentee's appraiser.

The mentoring relationship and dialogue associated with the mentoring process can provide a rich source of formative feedback for the mentee which can be used to discuss potential changes to teaching practice or developments in other areas of academic responsibility – such as planning strategies for developing a research profile.

EXTERNAL REVIEW

There are a number of sources which potentially provide feedback for us on our academic activities and teaching practice. External bodies such as the QAA have the opportunity to review practice – although this form of review tends to focus on process rather than practice. Professional bodies also show an interest in the quality of teaching and may offer feedback on the assessment and feedback that is given at an institution. Professional body accreditations tend to focus on subject-specific issues and coverage rather than on the quality of teaching.

A good source of feedback is from external examiners who are in a position to comment on both summative and formative assessment activities and the quality of the feedback provided on those activities. When externals have the opportunity to talk with students they can also get a view on the timeliness of feedback and the way in which students utilise the feedback that is provided.

GETTING FEEDBACK ON FEEDBACK

We can take the opportunity to obtain feedback on the quality of the formative feedback we provide, for example by discussing with students how the feedback we have provided helps in their learning. At the Open University, examination of the feedback is done independently from the teacher who provides the feedback (see Gibbs, 2005). It might seem a little strange trying to obtain feedback on feedback, but getting student feedback on the formative assessment activities and the formative feedback provided on these activities can contribute a very positive input to our understanding of the effectiveness of our feedback and, indeed, what it is (assuming that it is something) that students have learned from the activity.

It is often the case (as has been suggested earlier in this book) that student perception of the formative activity is different from the academic per-ception, and indeed, as Wiliam (2000: 15) surmises, 'there is considerable evidence that many students in classrooms do not understand what it is that teachers value in their work'. In order to improve the formative activities and improve the learning opportunity there is a need for staff to reflect on the effectiveness of the formative activity and one way of doing this is by obtaining student feedback.

WHAT TO DO WITH THE FEEDBACK

The question now arises as to what to do with this feedback (this is a question that your students may well have when you provide them with feedback). The important aspect is to reflect on the feedback and consider it as input into your ongoing academic development. You need to remember that feedback is only one driver for change and that there are other drivers, such as institutional policies, learning and teaching strategies, national policies and strategies, pedagogic innovations, professional body expectations, subject developments – the list goes on and on. However, taking the feedback in context and in terms of your academic and professional development, potential actions that may develop as a result of the feedback on your practice include:

- adjusting teaching practice as a result of feedback – you might consider what needs to be taught differently;
- change to assessment tasks or style of tasks;
- development of formative feedback approach – consideration of the timing, quality and style of feedback you provide;
- different pedagogic approaches aimed at engaging students – for example emphasising assessment for learning;
- opportunities for dialogue between colleagues – possibly leading to development projects or opportunities for research;
- using the feedback (could be subject or pedagogy) to lead to curriculum change.

SUMMARY

Formative feedback is not only an activity aimed at student learning, but can be used as a contribution to the evaluation of activities and as an input to staff development. The process of interpreting student perception and understanding of formative activities can provide a substantiated rationale for modifying teaching activities and practices. In this chapter the benefits of reflecting on how students respond to formative assessment and formative feedback have been considered and the ways in which we might make use of the data we gather from formative activities in amending our teaching practices have been discussed.

Teaching in higher education is a multifaceted activity and it is not possible, or appropriate, to attempt to evaluate teaching from a single evaluation instrument or mechanism. The mechanisms indicated in this chapter will help practitioners build up a picture of the effectiveness of their teaching and provide data that can be used to develop action plans for development and potential change.

There are many drivers for change in higher education, but feedback on teaching practice and on the provision of formative feedback can be a useful source of data for personal development, pedagogic development, subject development and even curriculum change.

Chapter 7

Case studies

CHAPTER SUMMARY

In this chapter a series of case studies are provided to illustrate a series of approaches to formative assessment and formative feedback. Thanks are due to all contributors who freely gave their time and expertise in providing their case studies.

INTRODUCTION

The case studies included in this chapter have been selected to illustrate a series of different approaches to formative assessment and formative feedback. So far in the text we have tended to focus on formative activities at a generic level without giving consideration to the differences between subjects and disciplines delivered in universities.

There are instances when it is appropriate to provide formative feedback which is subject specific, helping students to achieve:

- expected standards of the discipline; or
- required body of knowledge; or
- against professional body requirements; or
- against the subject benchmark.

On other occasions it will be more relevant to provide generic formative feedback, helping in the development of students' academic meta-skills, such as critical thinking, independent thought, professional and ethical issues, social considerations, sustainability or inter-disciplinary considerations.

Case study 1
FORMATIVE FEEDBACK AS PART OF STUDIO LEARNING

David McMillan

Mackintosh School of Architecture, Glasgow University

This case study is taken from the BArch Degree Programme and the Dip Arch Diploma Programme at the Mackintosh School of Architecture and illustrates the formative activities and formative feedback opportunities which can take place in the studio environment. Great emphasis is placed on constructive and formative dialogue between tutors and students, external experts and students, as well as between the students themselves.

The degree and diploma programmes consist of varying numbers of units, with a bias in significance towards architectural design studio-based projects, with other technical and theoretical supporting units that are increasingly embedded within the umbrella of the studio project. The programme is designed to reinforce a holistic approach to architectural design.

Stage (year) student cohorts vary in size from 70–90 in the degree programme to 50–60 in the diploma, with a teaching ratio of 1:14. This ratio reflects the belief in the value of the studio system and personal contact with tutors. Each of the five stages has one full-time academic stage leader and a studio team comprising full-time staff and part-time practitioners. They are supported by specialist and technical staff.

After an introductory stage briefing by the stage leader, a project descriptor (derived from the general unit descriptor learning objectives), outlining in detail the context, the building brief, technological requirements and deadlines, is given to students. The stage cohort group is broken down into tutorial groups of approximately 15 students to discuss general issues with each session lasting 1–2 hours. Thereafter, depending on the duration of the project, the groups would be smaller, probably consisting of five students, with the tutorial lasting 1–2 hours led typically by one or two tutors, with a subsequent period of individual tutorials lasting 20–40 minutes either once or twice a week depending on stage requirements. The tutorial is a discursive educational tool where both students and tutors may also simultaneously make drawings to clarify verbal communication.

Both group and individual tutorials are based in the studio to encourage studio use and generate a stimulating environment to work in. Group tutorials are an efficient and creative method that affords general discussion about common issues. At the end of each tutorial an indication of project progress and expectation of what could be achieved by the next tutorial is agreed.

At an appropriate interval there will be an interim review (students receive oral formative feedback) and at the end of a project there is a final review from which students will receive written feedback.

The review is a formal oral and visual presentation made by an individual, or group, to a panel of tutors including guest reviewers and the student's peer group. It takes place in a purpose-built teaching space adjacent the studio to encourage attendance by all students in different stages. Typically, to cope with the logistics, there may be four groups reviewing simultaneously, with each student allocated 20–30 minutes to present. The review panel usually consists of one or two guest reviewers and one or two unit tutors.

Traditionally, 2D drawings and 3D models would be arranged on a wall and its surrounds, providing the focus of the review, with the presenting student facing the panel and peer group audience.

At the review session the review panel strategically position themselves, the tutor chairing the presentation and compiling the written feedback (they may also time-keep and recap at the conclusion) positions themself within the peer group, with a guest reviewer or supporting tutor aligning themself with the presenting student, ideally forming a circle around the work. This creates a forum conducive to open discussion.

At an initial briefing by the stage leader for the guest reviewers it is made clear that peer group participation is to be encouraged and comments made by them followed through by the review panel to promote discussion and build student confidence. The briefing would also identify and clarify the objectives of the project, particularly for the guest reviewer.

At a pre-emptive peer group review students will have engaged with each other's work and this familiarity helps prepare not only the presenter but the audience, and is designed to identify strengths and weaknesses that can be addressed in time for the final review. These simple tactics help reduce the sense of confrontation and encourage a more creative collaboration between reviewers, presenters and audience. When the tutor is recapping the discussion (based on feedback notes of the relevant comments during the review), it is important that if it is felt that a significant issue has been misrepresented or omitted, then there is an opportunity for that to be raised by either students or tutors.

The student will also have nominated a student 'buddy' who takes independent notes of the review discussion so that there are two forms of written feedback available almost immediately after the review for reflection. Following the review students are encouraged to reflect on their presentation and this self-appraisal or evaluation will be brought to an interim progress interview at the end of each academic term (every 10 weeks, therefore twice) and finally at the summative assessment at the end of each academic year (30 weeks).

Ideally there should be provision for a debriefing session for the stage group between the conclusion of the project and the commencement of the next. This could be a period of individual reflection but also useful for raising general issues concerning process, content and learning objectives by the tutors, who may also benefit from feedback on the clarity of the unit descriptor.

At the completion of a unit the project is formatively assessed and alpha graded. The summative assessment at the end of the academic year, however, is where the final grading is awarded for all units completed during the academic session, when a student re-presents their portfolio of units which may have updated, improved or completed previously unfinished work.

Depending on the stage of study, the summative assessment is made by the team of stage tutors plus the specialist staff and programme leader who will look through all student portfolios submitted.

At the final degree and diploma summative assessments there is also an interview where the students present their work on the wall and are interviewed, usually by pairs of the stage tutor team, and this interview is reprised a few days later by external examiners.

Case study 2
THE INCORPORATION OF PEER ASSISTED STUDY SESSIONS (PASS) INTO THE CORE CURRICULUM OF A FIRST YEAR CHEMISTRY MODULE

Valda Miller
School of Molecular and Microbial Sciences, The University of Queensland, Australia

This case study has been kindly provided by colleagues from the University of Queensland and illustrates the benefits of peer assessment in formative assessment and formative feedback – through Peer Assisted Study Sessions (PASS). The case study also illustrates how formative activities can be applied to large student cohorts. The analysis shows that the benefits of formative activities in first year classes have ongoing benefits as students progress through their studies. The case study focuses on the incorporation of PASS into the core curriculum of Chemistry 1A (CHEM1012), introducing learning activities as formative assessment practices. As well as thanks to the author, grateful thanks to Elwyn Oldfield and Yvette Murtagh for their advice and recommendations. Many thanks also to Jeffrey Mak for his CHEM1020 formative learning task.

Problem

First year Bachelor of Science students at the University of Queensland form a large 1,500 cohort of which ~80 per cent, or 1,200 students enrol in the foundational course Chemistry 1A offered in semester one. The lecture based curriculum for this course is densely content-structured, multi-modular and multi-streamed.

While the curriculum was designed to give students the advantage of studying a large number of topics in separate modules within the one-course structure, it also had the potential to alienate rather than engage students. For example, any lack of coherence between teaching, learning and assessment may have been exacerbated unless there was alignment between course learning objectives and student learning. There was a dire need for formative assessment practices that would provide immediate feedback to students.

Weekly tutorial classes had been in place for many years, but were perceived by students as supplying information which was supplementary to the course material, rather than as an opportunity for them to clarify, consolidate or apply new concepts inherent in the discipline to their current level of knowledge. Failure rates for CHEM1012 were high, at 15–16 per cent (see Table 7.1).

TABLE 7.1 Effectiveness of initiative: student attrition rates

Chemistry 1A: CHEM1012		
Year	Enrolment Nos. (Grades 1+2+3)	% Failure rate
1999	1,279	15.2
2000	1,066	16.0
2001	1,040	6.7
2002	1,118	11.4
2003	1,131	5.1**
2004	987	4.9**

** Indicates courses with PASS in curriculum.

Rationale

In order to address these issues, the PASS programme was introduced into the core curriculum of Chemistry 1A in 2001. In this respect, PASS acts as a mainstream service by being proactively situated within this large, high-risk, first year course. The rationale of PASS as a learning model is that it allows the learning facilitators, or PASS leaders, flexibility to align student learning activities structured as formative assessment with progressive course assessment, by providing the scaffold within which leaders can design their own student-directed instructional tasks for students.

By addressing student learning deficits and by aligning these activities with course learning objectives, the supported study sessions in PASS also address two of the key issues to promote successful learning outcomes for students: curriculum development should include pedagogies that promote a deep approach to learning, and students should have the opportunity to self- and peer-assess throughout the semester.

PASS pedagogy

The structure of the PASS pedagogy is founded on organised hour-long, weekly, voluntarily attended study sessions for small groups of first year students, where student learning is facilitated by two course-competent second or third year undergraduate student leaders who reattend the first level lectures.

PASS leaders play a pivotal role in the success of the programme. They are responsible for creating the formative assessment tasks which fuel the inter-active learning environment for their students; one that is structured to meet their diverse learning abilities, needs and styles. Through peer and near-peer interactions in this study environment, students are able to admit ignorance and misconceptions and seek information, advice and remediation, without fear of jeopardising their academic outcome.

Because they share similar career interests with their students, leaders are also able to communicate their own appreciation for the discipline and thus act as role models, or mentors. As a result, students can gain confidence in their own ability to instigate learning processes and, by developing higher cognitive and effective skills, begin the transition away from learning depend-ence. By the end of the first semester, students primarily construct their learning within interdependently structured study groups within PASS, or more independently outside of the PASS environment, in effect forming small learning communities.

This framework for study promotes an environment where students are not afraid to question, critique and apply the concepts inherent within the discipline

– with enhanced student outcome. In two documented courses where PASS has been introduced, student failure and attrition rates have decreased, and an increased recruitment of students to related second level courses in later years has been noted (e.g. Miller *et al.* (2004)).

Student participation

Student participation rates are invariably high, ranging from approximately 60 per cent to 70 per cent of enrolled students; although there is a core number of weekly attendees, numbers may vary, depending largely on students' inability to master a particular concept, especially if application is required in a forthcoming progressive assessment. PASS is generally regarded by attending students as a rewarding experience, chiefly in terms of its perceived academic benefits but also relating to its socially interactive learning environment where students are actively involved in collaboratively based learning exercises. For most students experiencing changing lecturers, rotating practical class demonstrators and different lecture streams, the PASS environment is the one personally based, unchanging small-class learning environment that they experience in their first year of university life (see Figure 7.1).

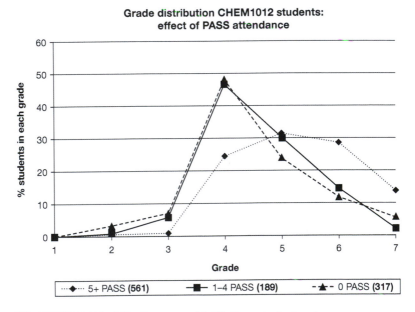

FIGURE 7.1 Effectiveness of initiative: student outcome

Effectiveness of initiative: qualitative student perspective
Student Feedback: PASS Evaluation: Semester 1, 2005

1) Have you found PASS to be a useful aid to your studies?
   100 per cent Yes responses:
   - It has helped me understand the concepts in an enjoyable atmosphere.
   - It has been most helpful. Thank you for running these sessions because they give me the opportunity to interact with other students and have my questions answered. It has really helped with my understanding.
   - You actually find out how much you don't know which inspires you to do study! PASS also helps to consolidate work.
   - It helped refresh the content that was being taught in lectures.
   - Yes! It's great. I go to two PASS sessions every week!

2) Would you recommend PASS to another student and why/why not?
   100 per cent Yes responses:
   - I would because it provides a relaxing, friendly, easy-going learning environment.
   - Because it helped me understand the course much better.
   - Definitely – it really motivates you to learn and helps you get to know the student leaders.
   - It helps you keep up to date with the work.
   - It provides insight into depth of knowledge required.
   - The relaxed, informal environment of small groups allows you to ask questions without being embarrassed, as lectures are so large and intimidating.

Success of initiative
PASS is both a student-centred and student-directed learning model whose strength is focused on providing self- and peer-formative assessment practice and immediate feedback to students within an interactive and supportive learning environment. Table 7.2 shows the positive impact of participation in PASS, illustrating the resulting improvement in student numbers in 2002, 2003 and 2004. This is particularly apparent for the students who took Chemistry in the first semester. PASS is ideally positioned within the teaching, learning and assessment continuum so that learning keeps pace with delivery of the course material. As such, student leaders facilitate and guide the learning processes of students to ensure that course teaching and learning objectives are aligned with progressive summative assessment tasks as they occur during the semester.

115

TABLE 7.2 Effectiveness of initiative: student recruitment

Recruitment of science students: 2nd, 3rd level Chemistry 1999–2004

Students in 1st, 2nd and 3rd level Chemistry courses

Chemistry level	1999		2000		2001		2002		2003		2004	
	1	2	1	2	1	2	1	2	1	2	1	2
1st semester	1,279	1,029	1,165	874	1,126	973	1,125	1,073	1,228	1,106	1,160	1,074
1st year	**2,308**		**2,039**		**2,099**		**2,353**		**2,334**		**2,234**	
2nd semester			110	95	87	106	148*	177*	173*	178*	200*	169*
2nd year			**205**		**193**		**325***		**351***		**369***	
3rd semester					109	108	138	86	122*	145*	161*	160*
3rd year					**217**		**214**		**267***		**321***	

* 2nd and 3rd level students who were offered PASS in 1st level Chemistry.

Leaders also align the level of difficulty of the instructional tasks to target the diverse abilities and learning needs of their student cohort: from easy revision quizzes, to moderately difficult discussion-oriented questions, to 'challenge' questions which have the highest degree of difficulty. Figure 7.2 illustrates that attendance at PASS activities has a positive impact on average grade scores.

Other reasons that contribute to the success of PASS as a scaffold for formative assessment-based learning are:

- Formative assessment tasks are designed for small groups, not individual students.
- Prior knowledge and learning skills of students are addressed.
- A reference bank of previous leader-generated activities is compiled and updated.
- Activities are group/class oriented; there are no individually structured tasks.
- Reference to all resource material – texts and lecture notes – is encouraged.
- Learning activities cater for diverse learning styles of students:
  - Active and reflective, sensing and intuitive, visual and verbal, sequential and global.
- Redirecting questions and challenging assumptions promote double-loop learning.

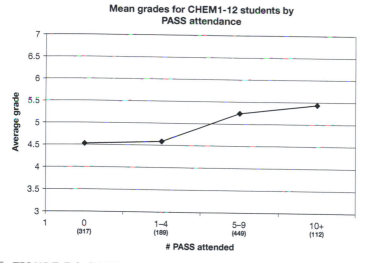

FIGURE 7.2 PASS attendance

- The importance of socially based, face to face, active learning construction.
- Having continual support and timely guidance from academic staff who:
  - provide formatively based questions and answers;
  - provide working models;
  - communicate with facilitators re: student concerns;
  - provide facilitators with practice exam questions and answers;
  - view learning activities prepared for module.
- Having support and supervision from coordinators.
- Feedback from students and leaders is used to fine-tune the effectiveness of each programme.

Personal reflections

PASS has continued successfully in CHEM1012 (now CHEM1020) since 2001 and remains a popular socially interactive learning forum where students are able to discuss key course concepts structured within formative, assessment based learning activities. Within the discussion groups, academically advanced students ask the more complicated questions, to the benefit of both themselves and the remainder of the group. Thus 'average' students are raised to a higher level of understanding, and students who are struggling with making sense of the course material will usually have their chaotic thoughts clarified and verbalised via other students' questions.

In this non-judgemental, small-group, team-learning environment, students are able to construct new knowledge, self-assess and be assessed by peers: an ideal forum for the development of generic and transferable skills. However, in order to foster student motivation and thus promote engagement with the discipline, it is vital for learning activities to be aligned with both course learning objectives and forthcoming, criteria-based summative assessment tasks.

Recommended course-based resource material, including online information, should also be available to students during the study sessions. Student outcome, evidenced by long-term retention and reapplication, is enhanced when students practise retrieving and re-presenting information from various sources, especially in the language of the particular discipline. In this context, current levels of understanding are also enhanced by critiquing and applying new information when constructing valid and personally meaningful 'big pictures' for each concept. Formative assessment tasks work well when structured as learning activities.

For this reason, it is important that leaders re-attend first level lectures and that regular meetings with academics are scheduled, where feedback and guidance underpin the alignment of teaching to learning. The structure of PASS is evaluated each semester and fine-tuned where necessary to maintain this alignment. Foreseeable future developments include collating an online repository of the leader-generated formative assessment structured study activities, which could also be used by leaders to access from remote campuses or for courses offered online.

Case study 3
FORMATIVE ASSESSMENT WITH LARGE STUDENT NUMBERS USING AN ONLINE ELECTRONIC FEEDBACK TOOL

Barry J. Beggs and Elaine M. Smith
School of Engineering, Glasgow Caledonian University

The QAA Code of Practice gives a good definition of formative assessment as having a developmental purpose designed to help learners learn more effectively by giving them feedback on their performance and on how it can be improved and/or maintained (QAA, 2000). Students at the University of Technology in Sydney have confirmed that well-designed feedback is developmental and supportive when they said that only the lecturers who really care about their learning provide feedback (see www.iml.uts.edu.au/assessment/feedback/). Work on feedback from Manchester Metropolitan University concluded that students wanted prompt feedback on work (preferably before their next assignment), sufficient comments to allow improvement and explanations they could understand (Dawson, 2006). These requirements of feedback are further reinforced by the SENLEF (2004) project (see Juwah *et al.*, 2004), which emphasises that comments on student work are only useful as feedback if students can use them to help them improve in similar further work. The majority of academic staff in universities and colleges face the challenge of providing high quality feedback to large numbers of students. There are various approaches to meeting this challenge. The case study reported here describes how one group of academics responded to the challenge by developing a software tool called ELF to aid the creation of consistently high quality feedback for large numbers of students. ELF has now become part of a comprehensive online student support software system called KELPIE see (*campuskelpie.co.uk*). A typical screen from KELPIE is shown in Figure 7.3.

In addition to performing a literature review to help inform the development of ELF, work was conducted to analyse locally produced, high quality, manually

119

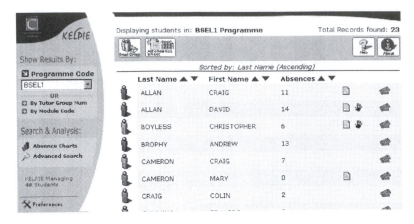

FIGURE 7.3 A typical KELPIE screen

generated feedback, which was known to be extremely time consuming to produce and difficult to maintain consistency with when large student numbers were involved. This analysis has been reported in detail elsewhere (Beggs *et al.*, 2005). The main objective was to develop a method by which the quality and quantity of feedback provided to students would be retained and possibly enhanced, and the efficiency and consistency of the feedback improved. One very important feature designed into the software was the ability for the marker to extract suitable feedback comments from a previously prepared library of comments and to insert appropriate text from this library into previously defined marking categories which form the structure of the marking template and the feedback report. The marking categories are selected to suit the assignment and the learning objectives. The feedback comments are selected to suit the requirements of the feedback to be provided.

The manual marking schedule and the real hand-written feedback revealed the basis of a range of marking categories and important content for the comments library. There were four obvious marking categories (with marks allocated to each one) and 27 different comments identified. There were several variants of what were clearly the same basic comments. The most frequently used comment was written by hand nine times. One comment was written seven times, three comments were written six times and so on. Thirteen of the comments were unique and were only used once. This detailed study of good feedback in action allowed ELF to be designed and implemented to meet the needs of the real world of feedback provision.

Rather than focus exclusively on this particular assignment for one subject, it was decided to try and discover as broad a range of marking categories and feedback comments as possible so that, from a very early stage, the software tool would be generic and would not be aligned with any particular discipline or type of assessment. Table 7.3 shows the generic marking categories identified.

TABLE 7.3 Marking categories

Category	Description
1	Introduction to report
2	Introduction to essay
3	Motivation, initiative and adaptability
4	Self organisation and time management
5	Knowledge and interpretation
6	Conceptual design
7	Creativity and innovation
8	Depth of understanding
9	Synthesis of knowledge
10	Group work skills
11	Technical competence
12	Application of theory
13	Discussion of limitations
14	Evaluation of results
15	Attainment of learning outcomes
16	Attainment of benchmark statements
17	Attainment of tasks
18	Process and keywords
19	Oral communication skills
20	Written communication skills
21	Use of diagrams/graphs
22	Main body
23	Word limit, punctuation and spelling
24	Referencing and plagiarism
25	Conclusions
26	General feedback

One very useful facility worthy of particular note is the automated e-mailing of feedback to each student after marking is complete. The marker is in full control of how and when this is performed.

In some respects it would have been ideal to use ELF to generate the feedback for the same assignment that the manual feedback study was performed on. This approach would have resulted in a time lag of one academic year and this was considered unacceptable. A formative assignment in a first year undergraduate module was selected for investigation. The assignment is one of the first that new students complete on entering university. The lecturer uses this assignment to provide key formative feedback in a number of areas. The assignment is a standard technical report on a laboratory investigation. The students produce the report as a Rich Text Format (RTF) document and submit it from their university e-mail account to the lecturer with the module code, their name and matriculation number in the 'subject' field. In addition to providing an opportunity for these junior students to receive feedback on good technical report writing, there are a number of other formative elements present in this activity. The students need to: use word processors to create a document in a format not normally familiar to them; access their university e-mail account (often for the first time); become familiar with the module code number; use their matriculation number; find the lecturer's e-mail address in their documentation. ELF was used to create a marking and feedback template by selecting appropriate marking categories. Once created, this template was reused for all assignments. ELF automatically inserts outline information into the template such as student name, assignment title, etc. A convenient practical technique employed during marking was to have the assignment open and displayed on the upper half of the screen and ELF open and displayed on the lower half of the screen to permit simultaneous access to both. Figure 7.4 illustrates this technique. The marker inserts appropriate feedback comments from the library into each marking category and assigns the mark. Free text can also be inserted. ELF automatically formats finished feedback sheets (including marks) ready for printing or e-mailing to students individually or in a bulk operation.

Some conclusions from using the online ELF software system to provide formative feedback were summarised by the markers' observations: 'I am not sure that I saved much time with this first serious use due to some familiarisation time at the start. I am very confident that the process is workable and will become more efficient as I use it a few more times. I can foresee ELF opening up some really important possibilities for making provision of detailed feedback reports to large numbers of students practical for the first time. Being guided by the library of available comments undoubtedly made my marking and feedback more consistent and I am sure helped me to avoid 'drift' as I progressed through the assignments. Students had no difficulty with the method and responded positively to the speed, quality and quantity of the feedback they received. I plan to handle the next coursework in the module, which is summative, in the same way.'

Further assignments have been processed in ELF, including the marking of project reports and essays in diverse subject areas such as nursing and engineering. In the case of nursing, very large numbers of students were given the same assignment and marking was done by a group of 20 different markers, each with around 20 assignments to deal with. Marking and feedback consistency is a vital consideration here. Figure 7.4 shows the layout of an ELF template indicating selected marking categories. Note that some of these categories are not directly taken from the list shown in Table 7.3. ELF allows users to create completely new marking categories if ELF does not already provide suitable ones.

Where time is limited or staff are worried about their ability to support reflection in large classes, the use of a reflective checklist can be very effective (Race, 2005). Students can be asked to complete this checklist after they submit their first formative assessment. The checklist contains statements that tease out best practice such as 'I made referencing easy by properly noting all of my

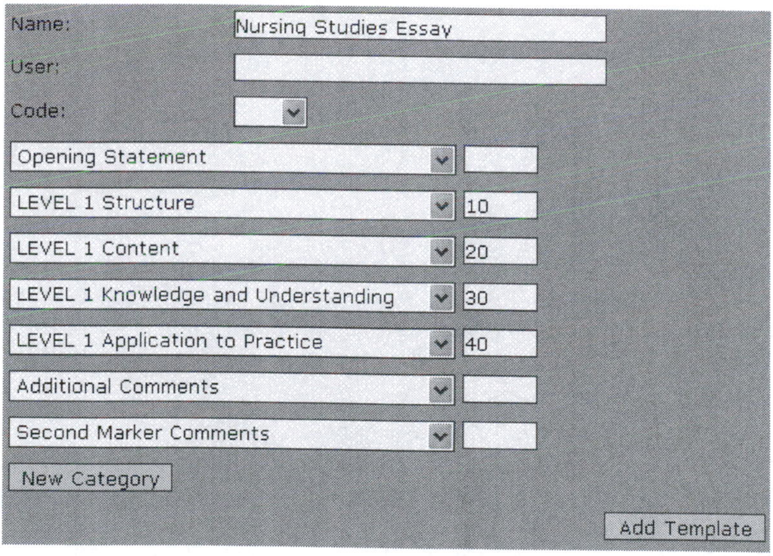

FIGURE 7.4 Marking categories template

sources as I did my reading' and asks the student to decide whether they had done this, would liked to have done it, didn't think it necessary or intended to do it next time. ELF is capable of effectively administering a reflective checklist when student numbers are large. No software tool can replace the skill and knowledge of a professional academic and it must be borne in mind that ELF is not some kind of 'magical' system that produces feedback automatically. It is a system to make the construction and handling of feedback more consistent and efficient – especially for large student numbers.

Case study 4
FORMATIVE ASSESSMENT AND FEEDBACK IN UK LAW SCHOOLS

Alison Bone
University of Brighton

This case study examines the use of formative assessment in a small sample of law schools in UK Higher Education Institutions based on research carried out in 2005 funded by the UK Centre for Legal Education (UKCLE), the law subject centre of the Higher Education Academy, based at the University of Warwick. The full report of the project's findings can be found online at www.ukcle.ac.uk.

This is not the place to attempt even a bird's-eye view of the history and nature of legal education in the UK today, but a little context is useful. Many pre-1992 'old' universities pride themselves on the nature of their law provision – it is holistic, often contextual and builds on the European tradition of a broad education covering e.g. the philosophy of law (jurisprudence) as well as the key subjects such as Law of Property and Criminal Law. Post-1992 'new' universities are often more pragmatic in their approach. Their student intake comes from a wider background and tutors recognise that although a large minority of the students may not wish to go on to practise law, they do want to cover all the core subjects, recognising the value of an understanding of the rules that govern modern society.

Along with many other HEI departments, law schools have seen a large increase in students in recent years and despite the increase in fees in 2006, this shows no sign of slowing down. Summative assessment is a necessary evil, but this project sought to discover if formative assessment was perceived as a time consuming, expensive luxury, the reasons why it was (or was not) used and the impact such decisions had on student learning. Rather than examining all the possible ways of providing feedback this project focused on formal formative assessment, i.e. coursework that was set and marked but that did not count towards a student's final mark in that subject.

There are of course many ways of giving feedback other than by formal assessment through coursework but the underlying principles remain constant. This project drew on the work of Nicol and Macfarlane-Dick (2006), who identify seven principles of good feedback practice that can help students to take control of their own learning. According to these, good feedback:

1) helps clarify what good performance is (goals, criteria, expected standards);
2) facilitates the development of self-assessment (reflection) in learning;
3) delivers high quality information to students about their learning;
4) encourages teacher and peer dialogue around learning;
5) encourages positive motivational beliefs and self-esteem;
6) provides opportunities to close the gap between current and desired performance;
7) provides information to teachers that can be used to help shape teaching.

These principles underpinned the data collection for this project, the key objectives of which were:

- An analysis of the different types of feedback provided to students on a typical undergraduate course.
- An evaluation of the effectiveness of feedback as perceived by tutors and students.
- An analysis of how feedback impacts on learning, taking into account the form, stage and level at which feedback is given.

The study focused on one subject so that there was some shared common ground. Contract Law ('Contract') was chosen as a 'typical' undergraduate law course. Contract may be taught at level 1, 2 or occasionally 3. Nature and type of feedback would, it was assumed, vary accordingly. In the event, all the Higher Education Institutions in this study taught Contract in the first year.

The research was primarily qualitative but within the tight time constraints (interviews rarely lasted more than an hour) both lecturers and students were encouraged to talk freely about feedback issues. Discussion ranged from how opportunities to provide feedback were (or were not) utilised to whether and how provision was made for students to 'practise' their assessment tasks both formally and informally.

In all, a total of 11 UK universities participated, including at least one HEI from England, Wales, Scotland and Northern Ireland. Both 'old' and 'new' universities were included. The sample represents around 10 per cent of the HEIs offering law degrees at that time. Interviews were held with 12 subject tutors. Discussion covered the nature of feedback mechanisms, their rationale and perceived effectiveness. A total of 65 students took part in 11 separate focus groups to discuss how and when they received feedback on their learning at their HEI and the nature of any assessment they undertook. They were also encouraged to discuss its impact – if any – on their learning.

Out of six 'old' universities, five set pieces of formative assessment. This was something of a surprise – it was thought that 'new' universities were more likely to set such assessment, whereas the reverse was the case. Only one of the five 'new' universities set any formal formative assessment and this was marked by the students themselves using criteria provided by the tutor. The students at this HEI thought this exercise was not particularly helpful.

Those tutors who set formal formative assessment were asked how they gave feedback to the students and their students were asked if – and how – it was useful to them. There was no written generic feedback provided by anyone. At one university the students said that the lecturer 'ran through the key points she had expected to find [in the work] during the lecture, but it was all rather quick'.

All students who did formal formative assessment were given individual feedback and in all but one university a pro forma was used. This was not perceived by the students as in itself good or bad – students were mainly interested in the quality of the feedback and this varied from tutor to tutor even within the same course, regardless of whether a form was used or not. Marks were considered by students to be as important as comments because students want to compare their marks across subjects and with those obtained by others.

Timing of feedback is continually stressed as being crucial both by 'experts' (for example Brown *et al.*, 1997; Cowan, 2003) and by the students themselves, and tutors who returned formative assessment within a few weeks were highly praised. Unfortunately, in two HEIs such feedback was provided so late that students felt it to be of little use – in one case they received it only a few days before summative work had to be submitted.

Key findings and recommendations

This study highlighted a diverse range of practices in a small sample of UK law schools. Clearly, the findings must be treated with caution, given the size of the sample and that it was based on just one undergraduate course, but the following key findings have emerged:

- More 'old' universities set formal formative assessment tasks than 'new' universities.
- The main reasons given for *not* setting such assessments are large student numbers and lack of time.
- No students in this survey were provided with any assessment criteria for either formative or summative coursework tasks.
- No generic feedback was given on either formative or summative assessment by any of the participants, although one university put up a 'model answer' on the student intranet which was greatly appreciated.
- Marks were felt to be very important by the majority of students in order to compare their performance both with other students and across subjects.
- Timing is crucial – feedback is generally wanted as soon as possible so that it can be used for the benefit of later assessments.
- Students who were not set formal formative assessment expressed a wish that they be given the opportunity to obtain feedback before attempting summative assessment. This was not affected by the fact that in most instances the first year marks did not 'count' for the purposes of degree classification.

The recommendations follow on directly from these findings:

- It is important to give students an opportunity to obtain formative feedback on their progress before they submit a summative piece of work. If large student numbers and/or poor staff student ratios preclude the setting of a formal piece of assessment there are other ways of giving such feedback (Black *et al.*, 2002).
- Clear assessment criteria written specifically for the piece of work to be attempted should be given to students at the time the assessed work is set.
- Feedback on students' assessed work should make specific reference to these criteria.
- Generic feedback covering the key points is found to be useful by most students and saves time for lecturers, who can refer to it rather than repeating the same remarks in detail on several pieces

127

of work. The jury is still out on whether or not model answers are a 'good thing'.

- Feedback must be prompt to be of any use. It is good practice to set a 'hand-back' date as well as a 'hand-in' date so that students know exactly when they can expect their work to be returned. Ideally the two dates should not be more than three weeks apart.

Case study 5
FORMATIVE ASSIGNMENT AT THE UNIVERSITY OF DURHAM: COLLECTIONS

Liz Burd
School of Computer Science, University of Durham

This case study illustrates the benefit to students of formative feedback as part of the preparation for summative assessment. Dr Burd's study also highlights the difficulties students face in taking responsibility for their own learning as part of the transition from school to university. The mechanisms, both formal and informal, employed at Durham are also discussed.

As part of the module regulations at the University of Durham all modules must contain some form of formative assignment where this work requires that students receive feedback on their progress within the module. Students will commonly obtain a grade from this work, but must additionally receive a form of feedback that allows them to identify where they have made mistakes so that they can facilitate their improvement. The format of the formative work set varies across modules and levels of study. Within Computer Science, students are asked to complete essays, short answer questions, weekly programming exercises and presentations. Students, as they tend to be very mark oriented, generally dislike such assessment methods and often fail to see the benefit until too late. The regulations in Durham, however, allow departments to make the completion of this work compulsory.

Probably one area of formative assessment where Durham differs from many other institutions is in its use of Collections. The Collections are formative examinations that are applied to all level 1 modules. Therefore in the first week of the second term (early January) all students will take a formative examination for each module for which they are registered. This case study will detail how the Durham Collections procedure works and the benefits that it has to staff and students.

Many students find the transition from school to university difficult. Furthermore, many institutions have students from a wide variety of prior study backgrounds. Some of these students, such as mature students returning to academia, may find this transition difficult. In Durham it is considered important that students in level 1 are quickly given feedback with regard to their transition into university life. The Collections procedures are intended to be a mechanism whereby students can efficiently be given this feedback.

Setting and marking of examinations

With any assessment exercise the overhead on student and staff time needs to be considered. Furthermore, it is important that for students the assessment exercise ensures that students learn from their experience. As all students taking level 1 modules are involved in Collections, an efficient way of organising the formative feedback must be found if feedback is to be timely.

Within Computer Science multiple choice questions are used. Questions are defined by the module team. For each module 25 questions are set for which students are allowed 1 hour to complete the examinations. Students gain one mark for each correct answer; there is no negative marking for incorrect responses. Questions have five possible answers and staff are encouraged to use a consistent style for the final option – 'None of the above'. To simplify the timetabling of this work, students take their examinations during the module's normal lecture slot.

The students' answers are automatically marked using the Formic system. The output that is passed to the meeting of the Board of Examiners identifies the final percentage attained for each student on a module-by-module basis and also provides statistical summaries such as minimum, maximum and mean marks for the module. In addition, a profile of the number of students who selected each possible option for each question is summarised. This provides an important profile for staff to analyse their courses and the students' understanding of each topic.

Meeting of the Board of Examiners

Once all the results are compiled, a meeting of the Board of Examiners is held to consider the results. The decision process that the Board uses is shown in Figure 7.5.

At the examination Board the examiners group students (for each module) into three categories. These are as follows:

1) those who have passed (gained a mark of 40 per cent or greater);
2) those who have failed by a small percentage (less than 10 per cent);
3) those who have failed by more than 10 per cent.

129

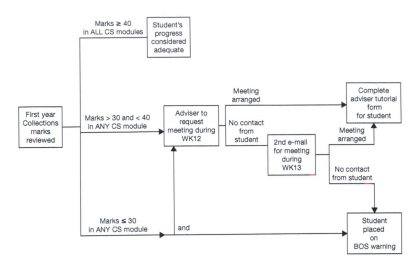

FIGURE 7.5 The exam board Collection procedure

After the examination meeting the marks are then revealed to the students. Those who have failed to attain the pass mark for any module (i.e. those who fall into category 2 or 3 above) are then considered further and required to be interviewed by their tutor and in some cases placed on a Board of Studies warning.

Within Durham all level 1 students belong to a college. The students' colleges are at least jointly responsible with academic departments for monitoring the students' academic progress. All Collections results are therefore forwarded to students' colleges.

Tutorial meeting

Any student who fails to gain a pass mark in any of their modules is required to attend an additional tutorial meeting. The purpose of this meeting is to diagnostically analyse the student's problems and to consider the profile of marks across all the student's modules. During this meeting feedback is given to the student, and the tutor and student collectively compose an action list. This action list defines how the student is to improve their situation and typically will involve changes in the student's work practices. These are then monitored throughout the year by the tutor.

Board of Studies warning

As multiple choice questions are used, on average students will get 20 per cent by change. Therefore, any student who fails to get at least 30 per cent in any one Collection examination is placed on a Board of Studies warning. This is a marker for the student, to warn them that they may fail the module. The warning requires them to see the Director of Undergraduate Studies as well as their tutor. In addition, the Department places specific attendance requirements on the student which are later reviewed in 4 weeks. Students failing to meet the terms and conditions of their warning can be issued a 'Keeping of Terms' warning. Failure to comply with the terms and conditions of this warning can mean that the student is required to withdraw from the university.

Other outcomes

Along with the Collections being a good diagnostic tool for students to gauge their early progress within level 1, the procedure is also very helpful to staff to gain feedback on their module. One outcome that has been applied in the past is that if a number of students are shown to be struggling with a specific concept, then additional support classes are provided to ensure that students are supported through their difficulties. New academic staff also find this approach useful as feedback on the suitability of their teaching methods.

Case study 6
PEER-ASSESSMENT AND FEEDBACK IN A FIRST YEAR BIOSCIENCE MODULE

Rob Reed and Fiona McKie-Bell
School of Applied Sciences, Northumbria University

This case study brings together a range of techniques and methods in formative assessment and formative feedback and emphasises the benefits and difficulties of student engagement in formative activities.

The formative activity is carried out within the first year (level 4) undergraduate classes in the Cell Biology module at Northumbria University, comprising approximately 200 students from a range of degree programmes, including Applied Biology, Biomedical Sciences, Environmental Health, Food Science, and Human Nutrition. This core module forms part of the first semester in year 1, and contains formative assessment components designed to assist students in the transition to higher education, including an appreciation of the standards required in coursework at university.

Context

During the first half of the module, students carry out a conventional practical class dealing with aspects of bacterial cell structure: due to a reduction in the amount of practical work in schools and colleges, many students now have limited experience of laboratory classes in the biosciences and a supplementary module in practical techniques runs alongside the Cell Biology module, to provide the required background skills (e.g. in microscopy, staining technique). The move from traditional tutor-marked practical reports to peer-assessment was originally driven by the rapid increase in student numbers, which led to turnaround times for coursework marking and feedback that were longer than the university's target of 2–3 weeks. The reduced amount of tutor feedback provided on each report was a further consideration, since this runs counter to the purpose of formative assessment.

Techniques involved

The practical schedule is a highly structured 'gapped' worksheet, with (i) sections into which students enter their basic lab results, together with (ii) follow-on questions designed to extend their understanding of the underlying processes and to challenge them to think more deeply about the meaning of their lab results. The marks available for each component are shown on the worksheet, giving some indication of the amount of work required on each aspect. The worksheet is completed (questions answered) in the fortnight following the lab class, and then brought for in-class peer-assessment.

During the in-class assessment period (1 hour duration), the overall process is first explained, including the purpose of the peer marking process in terms of its formative value, and therefore the need for students to *explain* the marks allocated with specific written annotation of the worksheet giving the reasons why marks have been awarded or lost. Students are encouraged to be fair and reasonable in their marking, to recognise the strengths in the work that they are assessing and to provide positive and encouraging feedback. Students then exchange scripts and are taken step-by-step through a marking scheme in the form of a PowerPoint presentation, with a slide for each of the marked components. The tutor explains each slide in detail, and sufficient time is allocated to allow discussion of any queries or issues that students might have in relation to allocating marks for any answer that might not be an exact fit with the marking scheme. In some instances, in-class discussion is used to take soundings of what other students feel is an appropriate mark in a particular case; this is useful, since it enables the tutor to draw out some of the more complex aspects of the work in a way that helps students to see that the allocation of marks is not always as clear-cut as they might have assumed beforehand.

At the end of the session, the worksheets are returned to students, who have 5 minutes or so to check over the feedback and marks allocated to their work before handing in the worksheets for marks recording. As this is a relatively straightforward task, the worksheets can then be returned to students in the following week's class.

Student engagement

As the task has a summative as well as a formative aspect (it is worth 20 per cent of the overall module mark), students engage well with the process. Students have the option to submit their work in advance of the in-class assessment session, for marking by the tutor – only a handful of students take this approach. Absence due to illness or other valid reasons is covered through the university's formal procedures for extenuating circumstances.

Before the assessment session, students are often initially apprehensive at the idea of putting marks and comments on the work of another student, sometimes expressing the view that such tasks are the responsibility of the teaching staff, or that they are not experienced enough to carry out the task. However, such comments then allow the tutor to explain how the process works, including the options of early submission or re-marking by the tutor, and to re-emphasise the value of the process, in terms of understanding the nature of assessment, and the level required to gain a particular mark. After the session, the students voice fewer concerns about the overall process, though several request that the script be re-marked, often because of the insight they have gained into the marking process, where they feel that their assessor may not have been sufficiently diligent in carrying out the process.

Improvements

The scheme has now run for over 5 years, and some important changes have been introduced. Initially, students simply exchanged their worksheets between different rows within the lecture room. However, in response to student complaints about cheating (passing scripts between friends on consecutive rows), there is now a formal system of allocation of worksheets (by numbered rows/seats) that avoids this possibility. In addition, scripts were once marked anonymously, but are now 'signed off' by the assessor, to accept responsibility for the marks allocated. Another important provision of the scheme is that a student who is not satisfied with either (i) the marks awarded or (ii) the level of feedback provided can request that their worksheet be re-marked by the tutor when handing in their worksheet for marks recording (around 5–10 per cent of students make this request, with only a handful of the worksheets being given a substantially different mark to that of the peer-assessor – these are all re-marked before the following week's class). It has also been found to be important to allocate sufficient time to provide opportunities to address the questions and concerns of students beforehand and during the assessment, so that they continue to appreciate the broader value of the overall process.

133

Reflection

The move from tutor-based marking to peer-assessment and feedback for the practical report was originally driven by increasing class size, and the consequent problems associated with providing timely and detailed feedback on coursework early enough within the module. However, experience has shown that this approach is likely to have greater formative value than the traditional approach: a 'feedback on feedback' study carried out with first year students has identified the slow turnaround of assessments by staff as a significant issue, with many students taking little notice of written feedback on coursework returned too late to be of benefit within that module (modularisation seems to cause many first year students to view each taught element in isolation, with little appreciation of the potential benefit of feedback in terms of 'carry-over' to subsequent modules). Such problems are avoided by this approach, which is timely and which also results in a better level of written feedback on worksheets, since each marker has 1 hour with the script. In the 'feedback on feedback' study, another request made by students was for more oral feedback on their coursework, with discussion on where marks were gained and lost. Given that aural learning is an important component of the learning styles of many students (see www.vark-learn.com/english/index.asp) the peer-assessed exercise addresses this aspect without the need to set up individual tutorials with staff.

Students gain considerably from this exercise: in terms of subject-specific material, they learn from being taken through a set of 'right' answers(including in-class discussion of borderline answers) in a way that would not happen if they were simply given an annotated worksheet, marked by a tutor. By focusing on the material for a whole hour during the assessment session, they engage more deeply than would be the case with a conventional marking system, thereby gaining a better understanding of the topics covered and reinforcing the learning gained from lectures. In assessing the work of their peers, students develop skills in critical evaluation that should prove useful in judging the quality of their own work in subsequent assignments. They also learn from the mistakes made by others, so they can avoid such pitfalls in their own work, and they also gain an appreciation of the standard required to achieve a particular mark, and of where their work falls within the spectrum of achievement of their peers. Having been initially apprehensive, most students are positive in their comments on this approach to coursework assessment in their end-of-module questionnaires.

The approach works well in year 1, partly because the answers conform to a fairly narrow range of options. However, the approach would be far more challenging for other assessment tasks, e.g. open-ended essays, where assessment involves higher level skills and critical judgements.

134

Chapter 8

Summary and recommendations

CHAPTER SUMMARY

This chapter extols the virtues of formative assessment and formative feedback as powerful learning tools, but also emphasises that they need to be relevant, be carefully considered and carefully designed in order to maximise student engagement and student benefit in participation. The chapter concludes with an indication of further work and opportunities for you to take your interest in formative assessment and formative feedback forward.

INTRODUCTION

The material presented in this book has attempted to get you to consider the role of formative assessment and formative feedback in your teaching practice and the impact that formative activities might have on the student learning experience.

Formative assessment and formative feedback are very powerful and potentially constructive learning tools. All learning and teaching interactions between teacher and student in higher education (and between students and other students) are to some extent formative in nature. Hopefully, this book has helped in raising awareness of the impact of these interactions on student learning and student motivation.

Providing feedback to students is an important aspect of the teacher's role in higher education. It is suggested in this book that feedback, quality of feedback and timeliness of feedback are key features in the student learning process and in the teacher–student relationship. Hopefully, we have promoted formative activities as being positive and constructive aspects of student learning and established that formative assessment can provide opportunities for formative feedback in a supportive, constructive and open environment.

Feedback is also a key aspect in assessment and is fundamental in enabling students to learn from assessment. Helping students to learn from their activities is a key aspect of feedback, but we also need to be aware of the impact that feedback can have in terms of motivation, both intrinsic (wanting to learn) and extrinsic (needing to learn).

OPERATIONAL ISSUES

We face a major challenge in addressing the workload associated with formative activities and in getting the balance of quality of feedback and timeliness of feedback right for students, in order for students to appreciate the value of participating in formative activities and for students to derive the greatest benefit to their learning from that feedback.

Many operational issues are imposed on us as a result of modularisation and providing our modules in small autonomous chunks rather than as a holistic programme of study. This has serious implications for the use of feedforward and the timeliness of feedback.

STRATEGIC ISSUES AND RECOMMENDATIONS

If we accept the assumptions that formative assessment provides a learning environment where it is safe for students to learn from their assessment activities without the risk of failure and that formative feedback enhances student learning, then the main recommendations and strategic issues we need to address (as outlined throughout the book) are that we:

- should reduce the amount of summative assessment;
- need to consider the impact of modularisation on assessment;
- must address the workload implications of assessment (both summative and formative);
- need to improve the quality and timeliness of formative feedback; and
- should encourage dialogue between tutors and students and between students.

MANAGEMENT OF CHANGE

In order to shift the emphasis from summative assessment to formative activities there needs to be a culture change. We need to reduce the amount of summative assessment, we need to encourage academic colleagues to embrace the principles of formative assessment and feedback and we need to encourage students to participate in formative activities and value those activities as part of their education and learning.

The management of change in any aspect of higher education is fraught with difficulty and certainly there are many challenges in advocating a reduction in summative assessment combined with an increase in formative assessment and feedback. However, the arguments presented in this book hopefully illustrate the benefits to students' education and learning from formative activities and that as such it is worth changing the existing culture of assessment.

FURTHER WORK

There is much work still be done in the development of techniques and methods for formative assessment and formative feedback and the implementation of those tools and techniques. Hopefully, work in this domain will continue the shift from a culture of summative assessment to a culture of formative assessment and feedback.

Associated with a shift of emphasis from summative to formative assessment is the need to carry out work to address student expectations of the experience of higher education and the value that students attribute to formative activities and the learning opportunities that can be derived from assessment.

As well as changing student expectations and learning culture there is a need to address the expectations of academic staff, HEIs and external stakeholders in the university system if the shift in emphasis from summative to formative is to be accepted.

OPPORTUNITIES TO FURTHER YOUR INTEREST

There are many ways that you can take your interest in formative and formative feedback forward. If you've got this far in the book we're guessing that you are interested in formative activities! For example:

- You might want to get involved in undertaking your own educational research into an aspect of assessment – perhaps utilising the principles of reflective practice or action research. You might even formalise your research – possibly through Masters in Education or Doctorate in Education or by getting involved with organisations such as the European Association for Research on Learning and Instruction (EARLI) (see www.earli.org).

- You could take the opportunity to integrate pedagogic research into your teaching practice.
- Promote learning and teaching research in your school and institution.
- Promote enhancement of formative assessment and formative feedback in your institution – an interesting web site focusing on enhancement can be found at Scottish Higher Education Enhancement Themes Initiative (assessment) www. enhancementthemes.ac.uk/.
- Get involved with HE Academy Subject Centres.
- You might want to take part in one of the development programmes offered by organisations such as the Staff and Educational Development Association (SEDA), www.seda.ac.uk.
- Alternatively, the professional body aligned to your subject or discipline might welcome your involvement in the investigation or development of formative activities.

There are many opportunities for taking your interest forward and the level of involvement is really up to you. We hope you take your interest forward.

 Time Out

▶ What would you like to do to develop your interest in formative assessment and formative feedback?

▶ Try to develop an action plan of possible activities.

▶ Who will you discuss your plan with?

SUMMARY

Assessment is central to learning and to teaching and is a fundamental component of higher education. It has been suggested in this book that there is too great an emphasis on summative assessment and that students and staff would benefit from a shift towards formative assessment. Formative feedback can be a very powerful learning tool when used appropriately and can act as a focus for dialogue between academics and students and between students.

Hopefully, the material in the book, the time out exercises and the case studies have encouraged you to think about and consider:

- the purpose of formative assessment and formative feedback when you design student learning activities;
- how students engage in formative activities;
- whether students appreciate and value the learning objectives associated with the formative activities;
- how you might reflect on your current teaching practice and how you might amend that practice to embed formative assessment and formative feedback to enhance your teaching.

We wish you every success in developing your formative assessment and formative feedback activities and we hope that you benefit and, most importantly, your students benefit from your interest in formative activities and your commitment to their learning.

References

Adams, C., Thomas, R. and King, K. (2000) 'Business students' ranking of reasons for assessment: gender differences', *Innovations in Education and Training International*, Vol. 37, No. 3, pp. 234–243.

Assessment Reform Group (1999) *Assessment for Learning: beyond the black box*, Cambridge: University of Cambridge, pamphlet 371.26 ASS. Available at http://www.assessment-reform-group.org.uk/AccessInsides.pdf, accessed December 2006.

Assessment Reform Group (2002) *Providing Constructive Responses to Learning. Effective Feedback: principles, policy and audit materials*, Cambridge: University of Cambridge.

Baume, D. A. (2001) *Briefing on the Assessment of Portfolios*, York, LTSN Generic Centre, Assessment Series, No. 6.

Beggs, B. J., Smith, E. M., Pellow, A. J. and McNaughtan, A. (2005) 'A critical analysis of assessor generated computer produced student feedback', paper delivered at ALT-C Conference, Manchester, UK, September 2005.

Biggs, J. (1996) 'Assessing learning quality: reconciling institutional, staff and educational demands', *Assessment & Evaluation in Higher Education,* Vol. 12, No.1, pp. 5–15.

Black, P. (1993) 'Formative and summative assessment by teachers', *Studies in Science Education*, Vol. 21. pp. 49–97.

Black, P. (1999) 'Assessment learning theories and testing systems', in P. Murphy (ed.), *Learners, Learning and Assessment*, London, Paul Chapman Publishing, pp. 118–134.

Black, P. and Wiliam, D. (1998) 'Assessment and classroom learning', *Assessment in Education, Principles, Policy and Practice*, Vol. 5 No. 1, pp. 7–73.

Black, P. and Wiliam, D. (1999) *Assessment for Learning: Beyond the Black Box*, Cambridge, Assessment Reform Group, University of Cambridge, pamphlet 371.26 ASS, available at www.assessment-reform-group.org.uk/AssessInsides.pdf (accessed September 2004).

Black, P., Harrison, C., Lee, C. and Wiliam, D. (2002) 'Working inside the black box: assessment for learning in the classroom', London, King's College, Department of Education and Professional Studies.

Bligh, D. (1998) *What's the Use of Lectures?*, Exeter, Intellect.

Blumenfeld, P. C. (1992) 'Classroom learning and motivation: clarifying and expanding goal theory', *Journal of Educational Psychology*, Vol. 84, pp. 272–281.

Boud, D. (1989) 'The role of self-assessment in student grading', *Assessment and Evaluation in Higher Education*, Vol. 14, No. 1, pp. 20–30.

Boud, D. (2000) 'Sustainable assessment: rethinking assessment for the learning society', *Studies in Education*, Vol. 22, No. 2, pp. 151–167.

Boud, D. and Knights, S. (1994) 'Designing courses to promote reflective learning', *Research and Development in Higher Education*, Vol. 16, pp. 229–234.

Brosnan, M. (1999) 'Computer anxiety in students: should computer-based assessment be used at all?' in S. Brown, P. Race and J. Bull (eds), *Computer-Assisted Assessment in Higher Education*, London, Kogan Page, pp. 47–54.

Brown, G. (2001) *Assessment: a guide for lecturers*, York, LTSN Generic Centre.

Brown, G., Bull, J. and Pendelbury, M. (1997) *Assessing Student Learning in Higher Education*, London, Routledge.

Brown, S. (1999) 'Institutional strategies for assessment', in S. Brown, and A. Glasner (eds), *Assessment Matters in Higher Education, Choosing and Using Diverse Approaches*, Buckingham, Open University Press, McGraw-Hill.

Brown, S., Armstrong, S. and Thompson, G. (eds) (1998) *Motivating Students*, London, Kogan Page.

Brown, S., Race, P. and Bull, J. (eds) (1999) *Computer Assisted Assessment in Higher Education*, London, Kogan Page.

Brown, S., Hartley, P., Ellis, R., Race, P. and Pickford, R. (2006) 'Changing hearts: changing assessment practices', symposium delivered at Northumbria, EARLI SIG Assessment Conference, Assessment for Excellence, Redworth, Co. Durham, 30 August – 1 September 2006.

Bull, J. and Stevens, D. (1999) 'The use of QuestionMark software for formative and summative assessment at two universities', *IETI*, Vol. 36, No. 2, pp. 128–136.

141

Butler, R. (1988) 'Enhancing and undermining intrinsic motivation: the effects of task-involving and ego-involving evaluation of interest or involvement', *British Journal of Educational Psychology*, Vol. 58, pp. 1–14.

Carroll, J. and Appleton, J. (2001) 'Plagiarism: a good practice guide', Joint Information Systems Committee, www.jisc.ac.uk/uploaded_documents/brookes.pdf (accessed March 2004).

Chamberlain, C., Dison, L. and Button, A. (1998) 'Lecturer feedback – implications for developing writing skills: a South African perspective', in *Proceedings of Higher Education Research and Development Society of Australia (HERSDA) Annual International Conference*, 1998, New Zealand.

Charman, D., (1999) 'Issues and impacts of using computer-based assessments for formative assessment', in S. Brown, P. Race and G. Bull (eds), *Computer Assisted Assessment*, London, Kogan Page.

Clarke, S., Lindsay, K., McKenna, C. and New, S. (2004) 'INQUIRE: a case study in evaluating the potential of online MCQ tests in a discursive subject', *ALT-J*, Vol. 12, No. 3, pp. 249–260.

Collis, B. and Moonen, J. (2001) *Flexible Learning in a Digital World*, Kogan Page, London.

Conole, G. (2001) 'Drivers and barriers to utilising information and communication technologies', London, IEEE Conference on Teaching and Learning.

Conole, G. and Oliver, M. (1998) 'A pedagogical framework for embedding C&IT into the curriculum', *Association for Learning Technology Journal*, Vol. 6, No. 2, pp. 4–16.

Cowan, J. (2003) 'Assessment for learning – giving timely and effective feedback', *Exchange*, Spring 2003, Vol. 4, pp. 21–22.

Craven, R. G., Marsh, H. W. and Debus, R. L. (1991) 'Effects of internally focused feedback on the enhancement of the academic self-concept', *Journal of Educational Psychology*, Vol. 83, No.1, pp. 17–27.

Cuban, L., Kirkpatrick, H. and Peck, C. (2001) 'High access and low use of technologies in high school classrooms: explaining an apparent paradox', *American Educational Research Journal*, Vol. 38, No. 4, pp. 813–834.

Curran, C. (2001) 'The phenomenon of on-line learning', *European Journal of Education*, Vol. 36, No. 2, pp. 114–132.

Davidovitch, N. and Soen, D. (2006) 'Using students' assessments to improve instructors' quality of teaching', *Journal of Further and Higher Education*, Vol. 30, No. 4, pp. 351–376.

Dawson, M. M. (2006) 'Effective feedback to students', ftp://www.bioscience.heacademy.ac.uk/events/wolv06/dawson.pdf (accessed December 2006).

Denton, P. (2001) 'Generating coursework feedback for large groups of students using MS Excel and MS Word', *University Chemistry Education*, Vol. 5, pp. 1–8.

DfES (Department for Education and Skills) (2003) *The Future of Higher Education*, London, HMSO.

Ding, L. (1998) 'Revisiting assessment and learning: implications of students' perspectives on assessment feedback', paper presented at Scottish Educational Research Association Annual Conference, University of Dundee, 25–26 September 1998.

Disability Discrimination Act (1995) with Amendments (2000) www.legislation. hmso.gov.uk/acts/acts1995/Ukpga_19950050_en_1.htm (accessed December 2006).

Eccelstone, K. (1998) 'Just tell me what to do: barriers to assessment-in-learning in higher education', paper presented at Scottish Educational Research Association Annual Conference, University of Dundee, 25–26 September 1998.

Entwhistle, N. and Entwhistle, D. (2003) 'Preparing for examinations: the interplay of memorising and understanding and the development of knowledge objects', *Higher Education Research and Development*, Vol. 22, No. 3, pp. 261–275.

Falchikov, N. (2004) 'Involving students in assessment', *Psychology Learning and Teaching*, Vol. 3, No. 2, pp. 102–108.

Falchikov, N. (2005) *Improving Assessment through Student Involvement: practical solutions for aiding learning in higher and further education*, London, Routledge Farmer.

Flowers Committee (1965) *Computers for Research*, Report of a working party for the Universities Grants Committee, UGC 7/635, London, HMSO.

Fullan, M. G. (1991) *The New Meaning of Educational Change*, London, Cassell.

George, J. and Cowan, J. (1999) *A Handbook of Techniques for Formative Assessment. Mapping the Student's Learning Experience*, London and Sterling, VA, Kogan Page.

George, R. (2002) 'The challenge, as seen by employers', keynote speech delivered at e-Skills Summit, Greenwich University, 29 May 2002.

Gibbs, G. (2005) 'Why assessment is changing', in C. Bryan and K. Clegg (eds), *Innovative Assessment in Higher Education*, London, Routledge, pp. 11–22.

Gibbs, G. and Simpson, C. (2004) 'Conditions under which assessment supports students' learning', *Learning and Teaching in Higher Education*, Vol. 1, No. 1, pp. 3–31.

Glover, C. and Brown, E. (2006) 'Written feedback for students: too much, too detailed or too incomprehensible to be effective?', in *BEE-j*, Vol. 7, May 2006.

Grandgenett, N. and Grandgenett, D. (2001) 'Problem resolution through electronic mail: a five-step model', *Innovations in Education and Teaching International*, Vol. 38, No. 4, pp. 347–353.

Haines, C. (2004) *Assessing Students' Written Work: marking essays and reports*, London, Routledge Farmer.

Hall, K. and Burke, W. M. (2003) *Making Formative Assessment Work*, Maidenhead, Open University Press.

Hamdorf, J. and Hall, J. C. (2001) 'The development of undergraduate curricula in surgery: III. Assessment', *The Australian & New Zealand Journal of Surgery*, Vol. 71, pp. 178–183.

Hattie, J. A. (1987) 'Identifying the salient facets of a model of student learning: a synthesis of meta-analyses', *International Journal of Educational Research*, Vol. 11, pp. 187–212.

Havranek, G. (2002) 'When is corrective feedback most likely to success', *International Journal of Educational Research*, Vol. 37, pp. 255–270.

HEFCE (1999) *The Bologna Declaration*, www.hefce.ac.uk/partners/world/bol/ (accessed December 2006).

HEFCE (2002) *Successful Student Diversity*, www.hefce.ac.uk/pubs/hefce/2002/ 02_48.htm (accessed September 2006).

HEFCE (2005) *Strategy for e-learning*, Higher Education Funding Council for England papers, 2005/12, www.hefce.ac.uk/pubs/hefce/2005/05_ 12/ (accessed July 2005).

Higgins, R., Hartley, P. and Skelton, A. (2001) 'Getting the message across: the problem of communicating assessment feedback', *Teaching in Higher Education*, Vol. 6, No. 2, pp. 269–274.

Higher Education Academy (2006) *Embedding Success Enhancing the Learning Experience for Disabled Students*, York, Higher Education Academy.

Holmes, L. and Smith, L. (2003) 'Student evaluation of faculty grading methods', *Journal of Education for Business*, July/August 2003, pp. 318–323.

Holt, R., Oliver, M. and McAvina, C. (2002) 'Using Web-based support for campus-based open learning: lessons from a study in dental public health', in *Association for Learning Technology Journal*, Vol. 10, No. 2, pp. 51–62.

Hounsell, D. (1987) 'Essay writing and the quality of feedback', in M. W. Eysenck and D. Warren-Piper (eds), *Student Learning: research in education and cognitive psychology*, Milton Keynes, SRHE/Open University.

Hounsell, D. (2004) 'Reinventing feedback for the contemporary Scottish university', keynote address presented at Improving Feedback to Students Workshop, June 2004, Glasgow, available at www.enhancement themes.ac.uk/uploads/documents/Hounsellpaper.doc (accessed August 2006).

Hunt, N., Hughes, J. and Rowe, G. (2002) 'Formative automated computer testing (FACT)', *British Journal of Educational Technology*, Vol. 33, No.5, pp. 525–535.

Hyatt, D. (2005) 'Yes, a very good point: a critical genre analysis of a corpus of feedback commentaries on Master of Education assignments', *Teaching in Higher Education*, Vol. 10, No. 3, pp. 339–353.

Irons, A. D. (2002) 'Using portfolios to assess learning outcomes in computing', in *Proceedings of 3rd Annual LTSN Conference on the Teaching of Computing*, University of Ulster, Belfast.

Irons, A. D. and Alexander, S. (eds) (2004) *Effective Learning and Teaching in Computing*, London, Routledge Farmer.

Irons, A. D. and Smailes, J. (2006) *Shifting Emphasis Toward Formative Assessment*, RECAP Guide, Northumbria University.

Joint Information Systems Committee (1999) *Adding Value to the UK's Learning, Teaching and Research Resources: the Distributed National Electronic Resource (DNER)*, available at www.jisc.ac.uk/index.cfm?name=dner_adding_value (accessed July 2005).

Juwah, C., Macfarlane-Dick, D., Matthew, B., Nicol, D., Ross, D. and Smith, B. (2004) *Enhancing Student Learning Through Effective Formative Feedback*, The Higher Education Academy Generic Centre, June 2004, also available online at www.heacademy.ac.uk/senlef.htm (accessed July 2006).

Knight, P. (2001) *Formative and Summative, Criterion and Norm-Referenced Assessment*, LTSN Generic Centre, Assessment Series No. 7.

Kolb, D. A. (1984) *Experiential Learning*, Englewood Cliffs, NJ, Prentice Hall.

Laurillard, D. (2002) *Rethinking University Teaching*, 2nd edn, London, Routledge.

Lea, M. (2001) 'Computer conferencing and assessment: new ways of writing in higher education', *Studies in Higher Education*, Vol. 26, No. 2 pp. 163–181.

Lea, M. and Street, B. (1998) 'Student writing in higher education: an academic literacies approach', *Studies in Higher Education*, Vol. 23, No. 3, pp. 329–338.

Liu, N. and Carless, D. (2006) 'Peer feedback: the learning element of peer-assessment', *Studies in Higher Education*, Vol. 31, No. 6, pp. 269–284.

145

Lunsford, R. (1997) 'When less is more: principles for responding in the disciplines', in M. Sorcinelle and P. Elbow (eds), *Writing to Learn: strategies for assigning and responding to writing across the disciplines*, San Francisco, Jossey-Bass.

McDonald, B. and Boud, D. (2003) 'The impact of self-assessment on achievement: the effects of self-assessment training on performance in external examinations', *Assessment in Education*, Vol. 10, No. 2, pp. 209–220.

McDowell, L. and Brown, S. (2001) *Assessing students: cheating and plagiarism*, Higher Education Academy, York, available at www.heacademy.ac.uk/resources.asp? (accessed December 2006).

McDowell, L., Sambell, K., Bazin, V., Penlington, R., Wakelin, D., Wickes, H. and Smailes, J. (2005) 'Assessment for Learning: current practice exemplars from the centre for excellence in teaching and learning', *Northumbria University Red Guides,* Series 11, Paper 17.

McGettrick, A., Boyle, R., Ibbett, R., Lloyd, J., Lovegrove, G. and Mander, K. (2004) *Grand Challenges in Computing: education*, Swindon, British Computer Society.

MacLellan, E., (2001) 'Assessment for Learning: differing perceptions of tutors and students', *Assessment and Evaluation in Higher Education*, Vol. 26, No. 4, pp. 307–318.

Marshall, L. and Rowland, F. (1998) *A Guide to Learning Independently*, 3rd edn, Melbourne, Addison Wesley, Longman.

Masi, A. C. and Winer, L. R. (2005) 'University wide vision of teaching with IST', *Innovations and Teaching International*, Vol. 42, No. 2, pp. 145–155.

Miller, V., Oldfield, E. and Bulmer, M. (2004) 'Peer Assisted Study Sessions (PASS) in first year chemistry and statistics courses: insights and evaluations', symposium presentation at Uniserve Conference, University of Sydney, Sydney, Australia, 2004. Available at: http://science.uniserve.edu.au/pubs/procs/wshop9/schws003.pdf, accessed December 2006.

Morrison, K. (1998) *Management Theories for Educational Change*, London, Paul Chapman Publishing.

Murphy, R. (2005) 'Evaluating new priorities for assessment in higher education', in C. Bryan and K. Clegg (eds), *Innovative Assessment in Higher Education*, London, Routledge, pp. 37–47.

NCIHE (1997) *Higher Education in the Learning Society,* The National Committee of Inquiry into Higher Education, London, HMSO.

Nicol, D. and Macfarlane-Dick, D. (2004) 'Rethinking formative assessment in HE' in C. Juwah, D. Macfarlane-Dick, B. Matthew, D. Nicol,

D. Ross, and B. Smith, *Enhancing Student Learning Through Effective Formative Feedback*, York, HE Academy, pp. 3–14.

Nicol, D. and Macfarlane-Dick, D. (2006) 'Formative assessment and self-regulated learning: a model and seven principles of good feedback practice', *Studies in Higher Education*, Vol. 31, No. 2.

Pelgrum, W. J. (2001) 'Obstacles to the integration of ICT in education: results from a worldwide educational assessment', *Computers and Education*, Vol. 37, No. 2, pp. 163–178.

Pelligrino, J. W., Chudowsky, N. and Glaser, R. (eds) (2001) *Knowing what Students Know – The Science and Design of Educational Assessment*, Washington, DC, National Academic Press.

Prosser, M. (2005) 'Why we shouldn't use student surveys of teaching as satisfaction ratings', Higher Education Academy, York, available at www.heacademy.ac.uk/research/Interpretingstudentsurveys.doc (accessed December 2006).

Quality Assurance Agency for Higher Education (2000) *Code of Practice for the Assurance of Academic Quality and Standards in Higher Education, Section 6: Assessment of students*, Gloucester, Quality Assurance Agency.

Race, P. (1994) *The Open Learning Handbook: promoting quality in designing and delivering flexible learning*. London, Kogan Page.

Race, P. (1995) 'What has assessment done for us – and to us?', in P. Knight (ed.) *Assessment for Learning*, London, Kogan Page, pp. 61–74.

Race, P. (2005) *Making Learning Happen*, London, SAGE Publications.

Ramsden, P. (1992) *Learning to Teach in Higher Education*, London, Routledge.

Ramsden, P. (1998) *Learning to Lead in Higher Education*, London, Routledge.

Rowntree, D. (1987) *Assessing Students: how shall we know them?*, 2nd edn, London, Kogan Page.

Rust, C. (2002) 'The impact of assessment on student learning: how can research literature practically help to inform the development of departmental assessment strategies and learner-centred assessment practices', *Active Learning in Higher Education*, Vol. 3, No. 2, pp. 145–158.

Sadler, D. R. (1983) 'Evaluation and improvement of academic learning', *Journal of Higher Education*, Vol. 54, No. 1, pp. 60–79.

Sadler, R. (1989) 'Formative assessment and the design of instructional systems', *Instructional Science,* Vol. 18, pp. 119–144.

Sadler, R. (1998) 'Formative assessment: revising the territory', *Assessment in Education*, Vol. 5, No. 1, pp. 77–84.

Salmon, G. (2000) *E-moderating: the key to teaching and learning online*, London, Kogan Page.

Salmon, G. (2002) *E-tivities: the key to active on-line learning*, London, Kogan Page.

Sambell, K. (1999) 'Self and peer assessment', in S. Brown and A. Glasner (eds), *Assessment Matters in Higher Education, Choosing and Using Diverse Approaches*, Buckingham, Open University Press.

Sambell, K., Sambell, A. and Sexton, G. (1999) 'Student perceptions of the learning benefits of computer-assisted assessment: a case study in electronic engineering', in S. Brown, P. Race and J. Bull (eds), *Computer Assisted Assessment in Higher Education*, London, Kogan Page, pp. 179–192.

Schunk, D. (1989) 'Self efficacy and cognitive skill learning' in C. Ames and R. Ames (eds), *Research on Motivation in Education*, San Diego, CA, Academic Press, pp. 13–44.

Sluijimans, D. M. A., Moerkerke, G., van Merriënboer, J. G. and Dochy, F. J. R. C. (2001) 'Peer assessment in problem based learning', *Studies in Educational Evaluation*, Vol. 27, pp. 153–173.

Special Educational Needs and Disability Act (2001) www.legislation.hmso.gov.uk/acts/acts2001/20010010.htm (accessed December 2006).

Stefani, L. A. J. (1998) 'Assessment in partnership with learners', *Assessment and Evaluation in Higher Education*, Vol. 23, No. 4, pp. 339–350.

Swing, R. L. (2004) 'Understanding the "economies of feedback": balancing supply and demand', keynote address presented at Improving Feedback to Students Workshop, June 2004, Glasgow, available at www.enhancementthemes.ac.uk/uploads/documents/postworkshop7reportvised.doc (accessed August 2006).

Torrance, H. and Pryor, J. (2002) *Investigating Formative Assessment, Teaching and Learning in the Classroom*, Buckingham, Open University Press, McGraw Hill.

Tuckman, B. (1999) 'A tripartite model of motivation for achievement: attitude, drive strategy', paper presented at American Psychological Association Conference, August 1999, Boston, MA.

Tunstall, P. and Gipps, C. (1996) 'How does your teacher help you work better? Children's understanding of formative assessment', *The Curriculum Journal*, Vol. 7, pp. 185–203.

Ward, R. (1999) 'Record of achievement to progress file', Appendix 1 to joint QAA-CVCP-ScoP Discussion Paper, *Developing a Progress File for Higher Education*, available at www.qaa.ac.uk/crntwork.progfileHE/contents.htm (accessed April 2006).

Wiliam, D. (2000) 'Integrating summative and formative functions of assessment', keynote address to European Association for Educational Assessment, Prague, Czech Republic.

Wiliam, D. and Black, P. (1996) 'Meanings and consequences: a basis for distinguishing formative and summative functions of assessment?', *British Educational Research Journal*, Vol. 22, No. 5, pp. 527–548.

Yorke, M. (2003) 'Formative assessment in higher education: moves towards theory and the enhancement of pedagogic practice', *Higher Education*, Vol. 45, pp. 477–501.

Index

Page references in *italics* indicate illustrations.

academic misconduct 48, 81–2, 94–5, 133
academic staff 98; expectations of 137; feedback on teaching practice 101–6; motivation 100–1; part-time ix–x; professional development 101, 102, 106, 137–8; research 9, 137–8; teachers learning from assessment 99–100; *see also* workload, academic staff
accountability 12, 13, 16
affordability of assessment 11, 20, 28
Alexander, S. 56
appropriateness of feedback 43–8, 86
Assessment for Learning (AfL) 27, 28
Assessment Reform Group 12, 56
audience for feedback 53–5
automated feedback tools and techniques 73, 90, 95–6, 122, 129; *see also* Information and Communication Technologies (ICTs)

Baume, D. A. 81
Beggs, B. J. 119–24
benefits of feedback 47–8

benefits of formative activities 20
bias 15, 26, 80
Biggs, J. 14
Black, P.: formative assessment 8, 17; formative feedback 21, 22, 23; formative feedback for academic staff 98–9; numeric marks 83; quality of feedback 45; student motivation 35; summative assessment 12, 13, 14
Blackboard 76, 93
Bligh, D. 77
Bone, A. 124–8
Boud, D. 79
Brosnan, M. 92
Brown, E. 10, 44
Brown, G. 11, 23, 36–7, 45, 57
Brown, S. 16, 36, 89
Bull, J. 92
Burd, L. 128–31
Burke, W. M. 44, 74
Butler, R. 83

Carless, D. 9
case against feedback 25–6
case studies: Mackintosh School of Architecture – Glasgow University 109–11; School of

151

Applied Sciences – Northumbria University 131–4; School of Computer Science – University of Durham 128–31, *130*; School of Engineering – Glasgow Caledonian University 119–24, *120, 121, 123*; School of Molecular and Microbial Sciences, The University of Queensland, Australia 111–19, *112, 114, 116, 117*; UK law schools 124–8
Centre for Excellence in Teaching and Learning (CETL) 27, 28
certification of student achievement 13
Chamberlain, C. 84–5
change in higher education, management of 21, 28–9, 33, 57, 90, 136–7; *see also* culture change in assessment
Charman, D. 92
cheating *see* academic misconduct
clarity of feedback 65, 125
Clarke, S. 77
'closing the gap' 44, 47, 50, 59–60, 65; good feedback practice 71, 74, 125; self-assessment and 56
Collections, University of Durham 128–31, *130*
comments: common 73, 81, 100, 120, 122; on draft coursework 78; unhelpful 85; *see also* marking categories; verbal feedback; written feedback
communication *see* dialogue
computers *see* Information and Communication Technologies (ICTs)
consistency of feedback 40, 84, 120, 123, 124
contradictory feedback 84
cost of assessment *see* affordability of assessment

Cowan, J. 21, 45, 57, 83
Craven, R. G. 83
criteria, assessment 38, 44, 64, 80, 81, 127
culture change in assessment 28–9, 30, 51, 136–7; *see also* change in higher education, management of

databank of common phrases and comments 73, 120, 122
Davidovitch, N. 102
Dearing Report 67
demands on academic staff *see* workload, academic staff
demands on students 34
design of formative activities 52–3, 58–63, 72
desire to learn 36; *see also* motivation
dialogue 8, 17, 44, 136; case against feedback 25, 26; about feedback 39, 48–50; feedback as catalyst for 45–6; feedback from students through 103; formative activities and 52, 62, 63–4; good feedback practice 70, 125; in lecture sessions 77; portfolios and 81; in practical sessions 77–8; in a studio environment 109–10; between teaching colleagues 104, 106; using ICTs to encourage 92, 93
differences between summative and formative assessment 19–21
discussion 63, 110; online 92, 93, 94; *see also* dialogue
diversity among students 9, 10, 33, 34, 51; inclusiveness 65–6; learning styles 117; surveys and 102; use of ICTs and 90

e-assessment 92
effective feedback, developing 64–5

e-learning 88–91, 118, 119, *120*;
   see also Information and
   Communication Technologies
   (ICTs)
electronic whiteboards 96
ELF software system 119–24, *120,
   121, 123*
e-mail 94, 122
employability 66, 67
end of module assessments 61, 79
enhancement of teaching practice
   10
Entwhistle, D. 16
Entwhistle, N. 16
equity 15, 26, 40, 66, 73
examinations 14, 24–5, 78–9, 92,
   128, 129–31, *130*
expectations, academic staff 137;
   see also academic staff
expectations, student 2–3, 40, 137
experiential learning 18, 66
external examiners 54, 55, 59, 101,
   105, 111
extrinsic motivation 2, 36, 37, 136;
   see also motivation

fairness 15, 26, 40, 60, 73
Falchikov, N. 13, 14, 79
fatigue, feedback 103
feedback 7, 20; case against 25–6;
   developing effective 64–5; on
   feedback 49–50, 55, 105–6,
   125–7, 134; motivating effect of
   37–8; purpose of 53–5; on
   teaching practice 101–6, 131;
   why students want 43–8; *see also*
   formative feedback
feedback charts and sheets *64*, 73,
   81; *see also* marking categories
feedback techniques: good practice
   74–82; types to avoid 82–5
feedforward 20, 24, 59–60, 61, 63,
   65, 136; defined 7; good feedback
   practice 74

feedout 20
formative activities 56–7, 77–8;
   design of 52–3, 58–63, 72;
   encouraging student participation
   in 41–3
formative assessment 16–19; defined
   7–8, 119; differences between
   summative assessment and 19–21;
   as preparation for summative
   assessment 60–1
formative feedback 21–3; defined 7,
   21–2; framework for providing
   38–9; generic versus subject
   specific 108; types of 59; *see also*
   feedback
Fullan, M. G. 29

generic comments 73, 81, 100,
   120
generic formative feedback 108,
   127
generic marking categories 120,
   121
George, J. 21
George, R. 89
Gibbs, G. 11, 20, 28, 33, 46, 57
Glasgow Caledonian University
   119–24, *120, 121, 123*
Glasgow University 109–11
Glover, C. 10, 44
goals 22, 23, 36, 74; *see also* learning
   objectives
good feedback practice 70–1, 74–82,
   125
government 12, 33, 88–9, 90, 100
Grandgenett, D. 94
Grandgenett, N. 94
guidance tutorials 68; *see also*
   tutorials

Haines, C. 38–9
Hall, J. C. 36
Hall, K. 44, 74
Hamdorf, J. 36

Hattie, J. A. 22, 47
Havranek, G. 60
Higgins, R. 46, 49
Higher Education Academy 65, 70, 124
higher education environment 33; *see also* learning environment
Higher Education Funding Council for England (HEFCE) 88, 89, 100
Higher Education Statistics Agency (HESA) 33
holistic curriculum 15, 20, 24, 60, 109, 124, 136
Holt, R. 94
Hounsell, D. 21–2

ICTs *see* Information and Communication Technologies (ICTs)
importance of assessment 11; *see also* purpose of assessment
inclusiveness 65–6, 104
independent learning 18, 47, 66
Information and Communication Technologies (ICTs) 73, 75, 87–97; academic misconduct and 82; ELF software system 119–24, *120, 121, 123*; examples of usage in formative assessment and feedback 93–6; multiple choice questions 76, 129; reasons for using in formative assessment and feedback 90
intrinsic motivation 2, 36, 37, 136; *see also* motivation
Irons, A. D. 56, 67, 81

judgement culture 8, 11
Juwah, C. 70, 76, 119

KELPIE 119, *120*
Knight, P. 11, 17–18, 19, 20, 59
Kolb, D. A. 18, 66–7

lack of feedback 83
language of feedback 60, 74, 77; *see also* comments
large student numbers 111, 112, 119–24, 127, 134; *see also* mass higher education; staff student ratio (SSR)
Laurillard, D. 92
law schools, UK 124–8
Lea, M. 44, 60
learning environment 33–4, 102, 136; dialogue 48–50; encouraging student participation in formative activities 41–3; feedback 43–8; of PASS *114*, 115; student expectations 40; student motivations and drivers 35–40
learning objectives 22, 23, 62, 118; *see also* goals
learning outcomes *64*, 73, 74, 81
lecture sessions, formative activities in 77
levels, types of assessment at different 21, 111, 134
library of comments 73, 120, 122
literature on assessment 6; formative assessment 16–19; formative feedback 21–3, 38; problems with summative assessment 14–16; purpose of assessment 11–13
literature on the impact of ICTs in education 90–1
Liu, N. 9
Lunsford, R. 56

McDonald, B. 79
McDowell, L. 27
Macfarlane-Dick, D. 24, 42, 46; dialogue 44, 49; feedback quality 45, 55–6; good feedback practice 125
McGettrick, A. 89
McKie-Bell, F. 131–4

Mackintosh School of Architecture – Glasgow University 109–11
MacLellan, E. 45
McMillan, D. 109–11
management in HEIs 27–8
marking categories 120, *121*, 122, *123*; *see also* feedback charts and sheets
marks 83–4, 126, 127, 128, 129, *130*, 132–4
Masi, A. C. 91
mass higher education 9, 33, 65, 124; *see also* large student numbers
mentoring 101, 104–5, 113
Miller, V. 111–19
model solutions 75–6, 127, 128
modularisation 15, 20, 24, 34, 57, 60, 63, 136; case studies 134; transferable skills and 68
Morrison, K. 28
motivation 8, 18, 47, 69; of academic staff 100–1; feedback from students 102; good feedback practice 71, 74–5, 125; intrinsic and extrinsic 2, 36, 37, 136; PASS 115, 118; possible demotivating impact of assessment 12, 50; student motivations and drivers 35–40, 51
multiple choice questions (MCQs) 76–7, 129

National Disability Team 65
Nicol, D. 24, 42, 46; dialogue 44, 49; feedback quality 45, 55–6; good feedback practice 125
Northumbria University 27, 28, 78, 131–4
numeric marks 83–4; *see also* marks

objectives *see* learning objectives
online discussions 92, 93, 94

online learning *see* e-learning
opportunities for giving feedback 2

part-time teachers ix–x
peer-assessment 18, 23, 56, 63, 69, 79–80; encouraging dialogue through 50; in a first year bioscience module 132–4; online 90; reducing workload through 27, 72, 80; in a studio environment 110; *see also* Peer Assisted Study Sessions (PASS); peer observation, academic staff
Peer Assisted Study Sessions (PASS) 111–19, *112, 114, 116, 117*
peer observation, academic staff 101, 103–4
Pelligrino, J. W. 12, 14, 21, 78
Personal Development Plans (PDPs) 18, 48, 63, 67–8, 69
Personal Response System (PRS) 95
plagiarism 48, 81–2, 94–5
policy, government 12, 33, 88–9, 90, 100; *see also* government
portfolios 81, 111
power relationship between teachers and students 25–6
practical sessions 77–8
problems associated with feedback 25–6
problems with summative assessment 14–16; *see also* summative assessment
professional development, academic staff 101, 102, 106, 137–8; *see also* academic staff
Prosser, M. 102
Pryor, J. 16, 17
purpose of assessment 11–14
purpose of feedback 53–5

Quality Assurance Agency (QAA) for Higher Education 22, 119

quality of feedback 45, 53, 55–6, 62, 69, 135; academic staff motivation and 101; balancing timeliness and 1, 83, 136; ELF software system 120, 123; feedback on 49, 105; good feedback practice 125; ICTs and 97; student expectations and 40

quality of teaching, measuring 13, 102–3, 105

quantity of feedback 53, 55–6, 62, 83, 120, 123

QuestionMark Perception 96

question/response banks 96

Race, P. 18, 36, 64

Ramsden, P. 33, 89

Reed, R. 131–4

referred students 61

reflective learning 18, 48, 66–7, 79, 110, 123–4, 125

reliability in assessment 11

report writing 122

research 9, 137–8

responsibility for learning, student 34, 56

reviews 110

rewards 51

rote learning 26

Rowntree, D. 12

Rust, C. 49

Sadler, R. 17, 23, 47, 81

Sambell, K. 92

samples of work, formative assessment on 73

scepticism about the value of formative assessment and feedback 3, 29

School of Applied Sciences – Northumbria University 131–4

School of Computer Science – University of Durham 128–31, 130

School of Engineering – Glasgow Caledonian University 119–24, 120, 121, 123

School of Molecular and Microbial Sciences, The University of Queensland, Australia 111–19, 112, 114, 116, 117

Schunk, D. 37

self-assessment 18, 23, 39, 56, 63, 69, 79–80; developing skills in 47, 76; good feedback practice 70, 125; in PASS 113, 115, 118; reducing workload through 27, 72, 80; in a studio environment 110; using ELF software system 123–4

self-esteem, student 71, 83, 125

Simpson, C. 11

skills, transferable 62, 63, 67–8, 118

Smailes, J. 67

Smith, E. M. 119–24

socially interactive learning 114, 118

Soen, D. 102

software system, ELF 119–24, 120, 121, 123

spelling and grammar 44, 67, 74, 85

staff, academic see academic staff

staff student ratio (SSR) 9, 90, 127; see also large student numbers

stakeholders in assessment 2, 28–9, 137

standards, monitoring 12, 13, 40

Stefani, L. A. J. 21, 47

Stevens, D. 92

Street, B. 44, 60

Student Enhanced Learning Through Effective Feedback (SENLEF) 70–1, 76, 119

student learning environment
see learning environment
student participation in formative
activities, encouraging 41–3
students: demands on 34;
expectations 2–3, 40, 137;
experience 10; feedback and
43–8; feedback from 101,
102–3, 105–6; large numbers
of 111, 112, 119–24, 127, 134;
learning opportunities 28;
motivations and drivers 35–40;
PASS leaders 113, 115; referred
61; relationship between teachers
and 25–6; self-esteem 71, 83,
125; thoughts about assessment
76; see also diversity among
students; peer-assessment; self-
assessment
studio learning 109–11
study sessions 113
subject specific formative feedback
108
summative assessment: defined 7;
differences between formative
assessment and 19–21; emphasis
on 8, 10, 29, 41, 139; formative
assessment as preparation for
60–1; formative feedback on
23–5, 61, 74–5; in law schools
124, 127; problems with 14–16;
purpose of 11–13; reducing 72,
136–7; in studio learning 111;
see also examinations; marks
surveys, student 102
Swing, R. L. 25, 101

teaching practice, feedback on
101–6, 131
teaching pressures 9; see also
workload, academic staff
techniques, formative assessment
and feedback 70–86; balancing
workload and 71–3; examples

of good practice 74–82; examples
of not so good practice 82–5
technology see Information and
Communication Technologies
(ICTs)
testing culture 8; see also
examinations; summative
assessment
tick box sheets 64, 73, 81
timeliness of feedback 45, 53, 57,
62, 64, 69, 135; balancing quality
and 1, 83, 136; peer assessment
and 134; summative assessment
and 24; in UK law schools case
study 126, 127, 128; using ICTs
92, 97
time out sessions 5; academic staff
motivation 100; e-learning 91;
enhancement 10; feedback 22,
54, 66; good feedback practice
82; problems with summative
assessment 15; professional
development 138; purpose of
assessment 14; referred students
61; self- and peer-assessment 80;
student learning environment
35, 39, 42, 47, 48; unhelpful
comments 85; workload issues
26
Torrance, H. 16, 17
transferable skills 62, 63, 67–8,
118
Tuckman, B. 57
tutorials 68, 109, 130

understandability of feedback 43–4,
62
unhelpful feedback 84–5
United Kingdom law schools
124–8
University of Durham 128–31, 130
University of Queensland, Australia
111–19, 112, 114, 116, 117
usability of assessment 20, 62

validity of assessment 11, 73
value of formative activities 53, 57, 62
verbal feedback 8, 55, 84, 134
Virtual Learning Environments
   (VLEs) 93–4

White Paper on Higher Education,
   HEFCE 88, 89, 100
Wiliam, D.: formative assessment 8,
   17; formative feedback 21;
   formative feedback for academic
   staff 98–9; quality of feedback 45;
   student perceptions 105–6;
   summative assessment 12, 14

Winer, L. R. 91
workload, academic staff 2, 9,
   26–7, 28, 32, 53, 62, 69, 136;
   change in higher education and
   28, 33; student self-assessment
   and 76, 80; techniques for
   managing 71–3; timeliness of
   feedback and 57; using ICTs to
   reduce 89, 91; *see also* academic
   staff
written feedback 19, 47, 55, 110,
   120, 134

Yorke, M. 16, 19, 32, 99

Made in the USA
Lexington, KY
30 May 2015